Paul Gayler

A Passion
for
Cheese

Paul Gayler

A PASSION
for
CHEESE

More than 130 Innovative Ways
to Cook with Cheese

with photographs by Gus Filgate

ST. MARTIN'S PRESS
NEW YORK

To my wife Anita and family,
with thanks for their continued support
and encouragement

First published in Great Britain in 1997
by Kyle Cathie Limited
20 Vauxhall Bridge Road, London SW1V 2SA

ISBN 0-312-19204-5

Gayler, Paul.
    A passion for cheese : more than 180 innovative ways to cook with cheese / Paul Gayler : with photographs by Gus Filgate. -- 1st U.S. ed.
        p.   cm.
    Includes index.
    ISBN 0-312-19204-5
    1. Cookery (Cheese)   I. Title.
TX759.5.C48039   1998
641.6'73--dc21   98-4170
                                                                            CIP

Home economy by Louise Pickford, assisted by Zoë Sharp
Styling by Penny Markham
Book design by Kit Johnson
Typeset by SX Composing DTP, Rayleigh, Essex
Printed in Singapore by Tien Wah Press

The publishers wish to thank Michael Day of the Huge Cheese Company for his donation of the cheeses used in the photographs, and the Guilde des Fromagers for permission to reproduce their logo.

Photograph on page 2 shows Red Mullet on Baked Salad Caprese with Basil & Olive Oil; photograph on page 6 shows Lemon Blini with Ricotta & Raspberries.

Contents

FOREWORD

In the UK, 18 pounds of cheese is eaten per annum per person. In France, the quantity is nearly three times as much, at almost 50 pounds. This disparity is revealing, and is not the result of French greed, but of unfamiliarity, even fear, on the part of the British. Although many enjoy a decent cheeseboard, too few dare experiment with the more unusual cheeses on the market, and even fewer branch out when cooking with cheese. Parmesan and Cheddar may well be familiar to cooks, but who has the confidence to know what goes with Stinking Bishop, kasseri, Port Salut or Taleggio?

In *A Passion for Cheese*, Paul Gayler gives us the necessary confidence to try out his inspiring recipes. With the same skill as that of a professional golfer—imagination, patience, timing, and conviction—he incorporates the cream of modern cuisine and the very best of international cheeses.

Paul has been cooking professionally for more than twenty-two years. In that time, he has won the admiration of his contemporaries by his enviable knowledge, his use of unusual ingredients, his hard work, and his impeccably run kitchen at The Lanesborough in London. His enthusiasm and integrity are as unforced as his cooking. As owner of the Huge Cheese Company, which supplies cheese to a great number of hotels and restaurants, I come into contact with many chefs and restaurateurs. In my opinion there are few better chefs in this country.

I met Paul 15 years ago when he was competing in the Mouton Rothschild prize and was searching for a Mothe Saint Héray. No cheese wholesaler in Britain even admitted to the existence of this cheese, a full-flavored *chèvre* from Poitevin, ripened between tree or grape leaves. Within two days, I had tracked some down for him and Paul was cooking with it. He won first prize.

The French have honored him, both for his skill as a chef and his delight in and knowledge of cheese, by electing him to the Guilde des Fromagers. As a frequent judge of cheeses at the Concours General and as the UK's only *Prévot* of the Guilde des Fromagers, I have likewise been impressed, and sincerely believe our pleasure in life and in food will be enriched by reading and cooking from *A Passion for Cheese*.

MICHAEL DAY

INTRODUCTION

My intention in writing this book was to put together a collection of recipes that not only demonstrated the vast number of superb cheeses now available but also exploited their versatility and character. I didn't want to write a book about cheese itself since, after all, there are many writers better qualified than I am on that subject. I confess that when I was young I didn't even like cheese. In those days there was much less variety on offer and most of it was mass produced. But during my career I have been fortunate enough to travel and, as I sampled cheeses worldwide, my enthusiasm grew.

In 1987, I was one of six chefs from Britain to be awarded membership of the Guilde des Fromagers, an association founded by several luminaries of the cheese world, including Pierre Androuët, and dedicated to upholding traditional cheesemaking in France. I was consequently invited to join the Confrérie de Saint-Uguzon. At my initiation, an elaborate ceremony took place after dinner. A procession of *maître-fromagers* dressed in fur-lined 14th-century robes entered, carrying huge baskets that appeared to contain France's entire cheese repertoire. These turned out to be rare cheeses from small farms, and I can recall their wonderful flavors to this day, each one in peak condition. I'd never before seen cheese treated with such reverence.

It seems to me that the history of cheese cookery has been one of missed opportunity. In Britain, cheese has mostly been banished to the cheeseboard, with a few much-abused exceptions such as Welsh rarebit and cauliflower cheese. The French have their classic cheese dishes, including soufflés and gratins, but they, too, tend to reserve it for the cheeseboard. Mediterranean countries are more comfortable using cheese in cooking, and the Italians in particular excel at desserts based on their delicious soft cheeses.

It is surprising that, to date, there hasn't been more effort to exploit cheese's unique characteristics in cooking. Why not pair blue cheese with white fish, or Cheddar with a lobster bisque? Use goat cheese to make a pesto sauce? Add Sage Derby to a stuffing for quail? These are just some of the unlikely-sounding combinations in this book that have turned out to be real winners. But let's not forget old favorites either. Where would we be without Gruyère scattered over a vegetable gratin, the salty bite of feta in a Greek salad, and cool, creamy buffalo's milk mozzarella with tomatoes and basil?

A final word: Although we are now fortunate enough to have access to cheeses from all over the world, I urge you always to buy local cheeses whenever you come across them. Better still, seek them out. Enjoy them on their own and then experiment with new dishes; you may discover your own great flavor combinations.

How Cheese is Made

Cheese could be described as an inspired collaboration between Man and Nature. Part of my fascination with it stems from the astonishing diversity that is created out of a single product—milk. Consider the sheer scope and variety of the world's cheeses. Then consider that they all are made from milk—many from cow's milk, but some from the milk of goats, sheep, water buffalo, and even, in some remote areas, donkeys and horses.

The magical property of milk that enables us to turn it into cheese is its ability to curdle. This is said to have been discovered accidentally by Arab nomads many centuries ago, when a bag of ewe's milk was cut open to reveal a curd-like substance. The heat from the sun had turned the milk sour, causing it to coagulate. Nowadays, most cheese is made from milk that has been pasteurized, that is heated to 162°F for just 15 seconds and then cooled rapidly to 88°F. This destroys the bacteria that cause the milk to sour and curdle, so rennet has to be added to induce coagulation.

Pasteurization is a controversial subject, with many cheese connoisseurs believing that a great cheese can only be made from unpasteurized or "raw" milk, since this contains the bacteria that contribute to the cheese's flavor and character. On the other hand, food technologists will argue that pasteurized milk is "clean" milk. This may be the case in factory cheesemaking, where milk is collected in large tankers from a number of different suppliers, making is difficult to monitor the quality of the raw product. But artisan cheese is usually made from milk produced on the farm, giving the cheesemaker complete control over its quality.

The uniform character of pasteurized milk enables the cheesemaker to achieve a consistent product, which can reach a very high standard. But the truth is that the majority of great cheeses are made from unpasteurized milk, although there are some surprising exceptions to the rule, such as Colston Bassett Stilton.

Besides the type of milk used, many factors influence the character of each cheese, from the pasture, breed of animal, climate, and even the time of year, to the way the curds are cut, the shaping, and the maturing process.

Once the milk has been soured, usually with a starter culture, rennet may be added and the milk clots into a fairly solid junket. This needs to be cut up to allow the whey to drain out. For softer cheeses, the curd is lightly cut and then left to drain naturally. For hard cheeses it is cut finely and then, in some cases, such as for Parmesan, scalded, or "cooked," at 105–130°F so that it becomes dense and more whey can be drained off. The curd settles at the bottom of the vat, where it is milled again into small pieces.

Other than the softest cream and cottage cheeses, all cheeses are salted with either dry salt or brine. Some soft and semi-soft varieties are also sprayed and washed with various solutions or with bacteria. Such measures encourage certain styles of ripening and the formation of particular types of rind.

The curd is ladled into suitable molds and pressed. Hard, compressed cheeses are pressed heavily, while the curd may be left to firm naturally or only lightly pressed for most soft and semi-soft ripened cheeses.

Unripened cheeses such as cottage cheese or fromage blanc are eaten fresh, but most cheeses go through a final stage of ripening, or maturing. This crucial process allows cheese to develop its character with time—from as little as four weeks for a Camembert to as much as four years for a Parmesan. During ripening, which takes place in a controlled atmosphere, the microbes and enzymes change their composition. Each stage contributes to the final character of the cheese and is carefully monitored by the cheesemaker.

Choosing and Storing Cheese

Always try to buy cheese from a specialist merchant, who will give good advice and, usually, allow you to sample what's on offer. Go for farmhouse or artisan cheeses, which tend to be far more interesting in character and flavor than plastic-wrapped, factory-produced ones. Whenever practical, purchase whole cheeses or blocks of a decent size. Small portions can lose their flavor quickly.

Advice on storing individual types of cheese is given below, but there are a few general guidelines to bear in mind:

The ideal storage place is a cool pantry or cellar, about 50–60°F. This idyllic atmosphere neither retards the flavor nor hinders any ripening process. Nowadays, however, most people are resigned to storing cheese in the refrigerator. In this case, select the least cold part and aim for a temperature of 45–48°F.

If you do store cheese in the refrigerator, place each one in a separate airtight container. Certain varieties, notably the strong-smelling ones, are best wrapped in foil first. Avoid plastic wrap as it makes cheese sweat. Any cheese sold in its own box, Camembert for example, should be stored in the box. I never freeze cheese, as all too often this gives it a dry, grainy texture.

Hard and Semi-Hard Cheeses

Hard cheeses are ones that have been heavily pressed to given them a dense texture. The hardest include the extra-firm Italian *grana* cheeses, of which Parmigiano Reggiano, commonly known as Parmesan, is the most highly esteemed. Wonderful for grating, the *grana* cheeses also include grana padana and pecorino romano, which is made from sheep's milk.

At the softer end of the range are the semi-hard cheeses, which include Tilsit, Danbo, Samsoe, Manchego, California's Monterey Jack, and Lancashire—of which the finest is probably Kirkham's Lancashire, one of my favorite cheeses.

Somewhere in the middle of the hard and semi-hard category is a huge grouping that includes three sub-groups: Cheddar-type cheeses, Gouda-type, and Gruyère-type.

Cheddar-type cheeses are cooked, pressed cheeses of middling firmness. They are prized all over the world for their sweet, full-flavor and culinary adaptability. Hence it is possible to find Cheddars of English, American, Canadian, Australian, and New Zealand origin. France's equivalent is Cantal. However, the only true Cheddars are the great English farmhouse cheeses, such as Montgomery's and Keen's from Somerset and Gospel Green from Surrey. Other cheeses related to this family are crumbly, piquant Cheshire (I am particularly fond of Appleby's Cheshire); very crumbly, mild Caerphilly, of which the supreme example is Duckett's Caerphilly; mellow Double Gloucester; orange-hued Leicester; and mottled-green Sage Derby, whose curds are infused with liquid sage extract.

Gouda-type cheeses are typically straw-colored with a thin rind and a coating of paraffin wax. Although Holland's authentic Gouda continues to be made in the town of that name near Amsterdam, other countries produce versions of it under an assortment of names—Teifi (Welsh), Broodkaas (Belgian), and German Gouda. Similar to Gouda is Edam, which is made from partially skimmed milk and therefore popular with those who count calories.

Gruyère-type cheeses range in flavor from a mellow nuttiness to a rich, full taste that is almost fruity and sweet. Their characteristic holes are formed by adding the popolonic acid bacterium. Swiss Gruyère has tiny pinprick holes spaced so far apart that they are sometimes difficult to see. Comté, Appenzell, and fontina have virtually no holes at all. The Norwegian cheese Jarlsberg has large holes, eclipsed only by the huge ones of Emmenthal.

Gruyère-type cheeses are invaluable in the kitchen. They grate cleanly and effortlessly, melt down rapidly and smoothly, and lend their fine, nutty flavor to a dish without overwhelming the other ingredients.

CHOOSING AND STORING

Even the hardest of the *grana* cheeses should be moist. The rind and surface should not be cracked, neither should the surface show signs of sweating. Avoid Cheddar-types that are darker near the rind or at their cut edges, as this may indicate that they have dried out. Never buy pre-grated *grana* cheeses: No matter how fresh they claim to be, the flavor will deteriorate within hours.

Grana cheese such as Parmesan that you intend to use for grating will keep very well double-wrapped in foil in the refrigerator. Hard and semi-hard cheeses for the cheeseboard should, ideally, be stored in a cool pantry, with the cut surfaces covered by foil and the crust free to breath. Failing that, store them as for *grana* cheeses for grating. They will keep well in the refrigerator for at least a week but no more than two. Bring them to room temperature before serving.

Soft and Semi-Soft Ripened Cheeses

These have a high water content and undergo a similar ripening process to the above. Soft ripened cheeses contain 50–70 percent water, are spreadable, and include Brie, Camembert, Bonchester, and Pencarreg. Semi-soft ripened cheeses, such as Bel Paese, Gubbeen, and Reblochon, contain 40–50 percent water and often feel springy to the touch.

Because they are moist and therefore more susceptible to microbes than hard cheeses, they ripen in a matter of weeks rather than months. Unlike hard cheeses, which are ripened from within by adding a starter bacteria to them, soft ripened cheeses are ripened from the outside, by the action of a surface mold that is sprayed on after salting. In order to create a bloomy white rind, such as the one on Brie, Camembert, and Coulommiers, the cheese is sprayed with the mold *Penicillium candidum*. The relatively mild, creamy characteristics of semi-soft cheeses such as Bel Paese and Morbier are achieved by washing the rind with a brine that slows down bacterial development.

Some semi-soft varieties, such as Port Salut, Münster, and Reblochon, are known as monastery cheeses because they are ripened by a method developed by Trappist monks. The rind is washed with solutions that include alcohol—usually wine, beer, or liqueur—resulting in a tangy flavor, savory aroma, and distinctive rind. Nowadays a culture of *Breyibacterium linens* might be used instead. This creates a thin, yellowish-red bacterial growth on the rind, which is not eaten.

CHOOSING AND STORING

Soft ripened cheeses with white bloomy rinds should never smell of ammonia, nor should their rind show signs of hardness or browning. The paste should not ooze excessively. Ripe, whole cheeses should feel springy to the touch. The paste of cut wedges should look plump and even textured; a chalky line indicates underripeness.

Semi-soft ripened cheeses, including the monastery varieties, should possess a fruity—but never rank—aroma and feel slightly elastic. The rind should look fresh and ungummy.

Store soft and semi-soft ripened cheeses wrapped—or in the case of monastery cheeses double-wrapped—in foil in an airtight box in the refrigerator. The soft cheese Vacherin Mont d'Or is a case apart: It should never be refrigerated. You should keep it in a cool, damp place and press a block of wood against cut surfaces to prevent them running.

Bring soft ripened varieties to room temperature two hours before serving. Once fully ripe they stay at their best for only a day or two. Semi-soft ripened cheeses such as Bel Paese keep for up to ten days, while the monastery cheeses vary in their keeping ability—from two to three days for Pont l'Évêque and up to a week for Reblochon.

Soft Fresh Cheeses

These are uncooked and unripened cheeses. Uncooked means that the curds are not heated in their whey—which would encourage them to harden and cohere—while unripened indicates that the cheeses have not been ripened for more than a few days. They are too young to have developed any rind. Most soft fresh cheeses are made from cow's milk, often skimmed of its fat. Examples include cottage cheese, curd cheese, fromage frais, fromage blanc, quark, and pot or farmer's cheese.

Fresh ricotta, one of the gems of Piedmont, is different. Traditionally it is prepared from the whey left over from sheep's milk after making pecorino. However, sometimes the whey from other cheeses, including cow's milk varieties, is used. Ricotta's dry, bland texture makes it ideal for blending with other ingredients in both savory and sweet dishes.

Cream cheese is, as the name implies, made from cream rather than milk. One

of the most celebrated examples is the devastatingly rich Italian mascarpone, which was originally made only in Lombardy in autumn and winter. It is created from cream that has been skimmed from whole milk. Once its curds have formed, they are drained for about twenty-four hours and then whipped to a texture like very thick cream. Mascarpone tastes delicate and slightly sweet and has a range of culinary uses, its affinity with fruit and chocolate being surpassed only by its empathy with savory ingredients.

CHOOSING AND STORING

These cheeses should look and smell very fresh, clean, and white, with no grubby edges. On no account should they ever taste bitter. Ricotta bought loose from a good Italian food shop or cheese shop has an incomparable sweet, fresh flavor that bears no resemblance to the type sold in tubs. It must be eaten within a day or two, though, as the flavor becomes tainted very quickly.

All soft fresh cheeses are highly perishable. If possible, use a cool bag to carry them home and then put them on the coldest shelf of the refrigerator. Very moist types of ricotta, cottage, and curd cheese benefit from being stored in the refrigerator on a draining plate covered with a bowl. The drier fresh cheeses, including cream cheese, can be placed directly in an airtight container—lined with wax paper or foil if you wish. Use soft fresh cheese within four days.

Pasta Filata Cheeses

Pasta filata is an Italian term meaning "spun paste" and refers to a technique of immersing the curd in hot water or whey, then kneading and stretching it. Well known *pasta filata* cheeses include mozzarella, a semi-soft, unripened cheese made with the milk of cows or water buffalo; provolone, a ripened cheese that is

available as a mild *dolce* or a stronger-tasting *piccante*; and Caciocavello, which is also ripened, often smoked, and can be just firm enough to slice when young or hard enough to grate when mature. All such cheeses are widely used in the Italian kitchen, especially for toppings, fillings, and stuffings.

CHOOSING AND STORING

If bought loose from an Italian grocer, mozzarella should have an immaculately white color and a fresh, lactic smell. Otherwise, buy the type sold in a little sachet of whey rather than the dry, plastic-wrapped ones. Buffalo's milk mozzarella is considered superior to cow's milk because of its stronger flavor and softer, less rubbery texture. Provolone should possess a faint, lactic aroma. With both provolone and Caciocavello, look for a fine glossy rind and avoid holes in the paste, as these may indicate internal fermentation.

Mozzarella bought loose should immediately be immersed in milk, kept in the refrigerator, and consumed within five days. With supermarket versions in their sealed bags of whey, honor the expiration date and keep any partially used portions in the whey in a dish. Store provolone and Caciocavello double-wrapped in foil. Provolone will keep well for one week in a cool place or the refrigerator and Caciocavello for up to two weeks.

Goat Cheeses

Ranging in texture from soft and creamy to dry and sliceable, goat's milk cheeses are now made in countries all over the world. In France, they are known as *chèvre*, the generic term for such cheeses. While they all share a dry, piquant aftertaste, their tangy—and unmistakably "goaty"—flavor varies in strength according to the region of production, altitude, ripening period, and mold cultures.

Traditionally produced on small farms or co-operatives throughout France and the Mediterranean, *chèvre* is made into a variety of small shapes: logs (*bûches*), dainty cylinders (*bûchettes*), little bells (*clochettes*), and an assortment of pyramids, disks, and so on. The name *crottin*—which, you may or may not wish to know, means horse droppings!—refers to the shape of the small, hard, round goat cheeses and also to their slightly darker coloring. Crottin de Chavignol is probably the best-known example and is highly prized for its bracingly sharp, full flavor.

In recent years goat cheeses have become very popular in Britain, Australia, and the United States, with many small cheesemakers producing their own unique versions. Montrachet is possibly the best-known American variety, while Kervella is produced in Western Australia, and Chabis, Golden Cross, Roubiliac, Tymsboro', and many others in Britain.

CHOOSING AND STORING
Because there is such diversity and seasonal variance within this group, it is best to sample before you buy. That way, you will be sure that the degree of tartness, ripeness, dryness, and so on is to your taste. Autumn and spring are particularly good times to buy, although crottin de Chavignol tends to be better in winter. Avoid tough-looking rinds unless, of course, you want a well-aged crottin. Don't buy cheeses with messy coloring or a rancid smell.

Many goat cheeses are sold slightly underripe. Bear in mind that they will continue to mature and will ripen quickly if left beneath a cloche at a room temperature of, say, 68°F. If you want to hold the cheese at a particular stage of maturity, wrap it in foil and store it in an airtight container in the refrigerator. Most goat cheeses will keep well in this way for at least a week.

Blue Cheeses

Blue cheeses acquire their characteristic veining from mold spores. These may be introduced to the milk before it is soured and then encouraged to develop during ripening, when the cheese is pierced with fine needles. This allows the air in so the mold can spread.

The most noble blue cheese must surely be Roquefort. Some 2,000 years ago it acquired its veining from the natural *Penicillium glaucum*, which thrived in the limestone caves of the Combalou plateau in France. In 1411, Charles VI bestowed a royal charter upon these caves, thereby initiating the Roquefort *appellation*, or quality control, which still exists today. Unusually for a blue cheese, Roquefort is made with sheep's milk, which is partly responsible for its pungent flavor. In cookery, its assertiveness works wonderfully well with other robust ingredients.

Italy's champion blue cheese is Gorgonzola, which is milder, softer, and less salty than Roquefort. Both cheeses have very little rind.

Britain's most illustrious example is Stilton, of which the finest is Colston Bassett Stilton. It has a distinctive rind and is moist and creamy. More recent British blues include Dunsyre Blue (cow's milk) and Lanark Blue (sheep's milk) from Scotland, and Harbourne Blue (goat's milk) and Beenleigh Blue (sheep's milk) from Devon.

Ireland's most famous is Cashel Blue; like Roquefort and Gorgonzola, it has a foil-wrapped rind. Its particularly creamy texture blends smoothly in cooking. Other soft-textured blues that cook well include the American Oregon Blue and Maytag Blue.

CHOOSING AND STORING
Choose Roquefort in its prime, that is from around six months old. In perfect condition it will have a creamy, moist, virtually white paste and a uniform greenish-blue veining. It should have just a faint smell of mold. These guidelines apply to most blue cheeses that are wrapped in foil, except their paste is not quite as ivory-white as that of Roquefort and some of them reach maturity at only three months.

Gorgonzola should be springy to the touch and never brownish and hard. Contrary to popular belief, it should not have a pungent smell. Stilton should be creamy-ivory, with an even distribution of greenish-blue veining. It should be open-textured and never dry, hard, or salty.

Wrap all foil-finished blue cheeses except Gorgonzola in a double layer of foil and keep them in an airtight container in the refrigerator. Gorgonzola is better wrapped in a damp cloth and stored in a cool place. All these cheeses should stay in good condition for 8 to 12 days. Be sure to bring them back to room temperature before serving.

The best way to store Stilton is wrapped in a linen cloth in a cool cellar or pantry. Moisten the cloth if the cheese starts to dry out. If these conditions are impracticable, store it as for Roquefort.

The Cheeseboard

The cheeseboard in a good restaurant will offer 10 to 15 varieties of cheese, chosen for their different characters and strengths. At home, it is better to have a small selection of cheeses in their prime than a large number in poor condition. A small selection is also less confusing to the palate, enabling your guests to relish each cheese to the full. It generally makes sense to offer one hard or semi-hard cheese, one semi-soft, and one blue.

If possible, buy from a good cheese shop, where the cheeses are properly stored and staff will be able to advise you. As a change, it can be fun to put together an alternative cheeseboard—see pages 183–9 for ideas.

Bring refrigerated cheeses to room temperature at least an hour before serving to allow the full flavor to develop. However, the prepared cheeseboard should not be left in a warm room for more than 40 minutes, otherwise the cheeses may sweat. One way of overcoming this is to put the cheeses on the board and cover them with a damp cloth. I like only wooden boards, and I provide a separate knife for each cheese to prevent the different flavors from intermingling.

There is an art to cutting cheese so that the cheeseboard continues to look appetizing and wastage is minimized. Small square or round cheeses, such as Camembert, should be cut in half (diagonally if it is a square cheese) and then into small triangular wedges. It used to be considered bad manners to cut the "nose" off a wedge of Brie, and it certainly leaves an unappetizing piece of rind. Instead, long slices should be taken from alternate sides so that it maintains its shape. Tall, thin pieces of cheese, such as a wedge from a whole Cheddar, can be laid on their side, making it easier to cut off long slices. Finally, truckles such as Stilton, need to have a "lid" cut off the top. You can then either slice off whole rounds or score a line around the cheese an inch or so from the top and cut down to give small wedges. Replace the lid when storing the cheese.

What to serve with cheese? I prefer something simple such as crusty bread and perhaps some tart grapes, crisp apples, or ripe pears. I avoid crackers and butter since I am not convinced that they enhance the cheese. Occasionally, though, I do like to serve a good chutney with a farmhouse Cheddar or similar cheese (see pages 186–8).

Here are my twelve favorite cheeseboards for the year. I have aimed for a good balance of texture, color, and taste in each one and have brought in seasonal cheeses at their peak.

January
Fourme d'Ambert
Explorateur
St. Marcellin
Cheshire

February
St. Agur
Wisconsin Cheddar
Port Salut
Bresse Brie

March
Vermont Cheddar
Montrachet
Epoisses
Brillat Savarin

April
Petit Reblochon
Livarot
Pierre Robert
Valdeon

May
Monterey Jack
Etorki
Neufchâtel
Crottin de Chavignol

June
Smoked Gouda
Muscoot
Colby Cheddar
Roquefort

July
St. Marcellin
Amelia
Wabash Cannonball
Brick

August
Montbriac
Banon
Vermont Shepherd
Explorateur

September
Edel de Cleron
Coeur de Lion Camembert
Treasure Cave (Minnesota Blue)
Chaumes

October
St. Paulin
Munster
Chaource
Taupiere

November
St. Nectaire
Tomme de Savoie
Tallegio
Wisconsin Blue

December
Stilton
Perail
Amram
Majorco

Serving Wine with Cheese

Alain Senderens, the well-known Parisian chef-restaurateur, regards the partnership of cheese and wine as so important that he displays a list of famous cheese and wine marriages in his restaurant. Ultimately, however, personal taste should play a part–although a few general rules hold good, such as strong cheeses need a full-bodies wine, while mild ones are better matched with a light wine.

One common fallacy that I am happy to ignore is that all cheese goes with all red wine. This isn't the case. You must take into account the individual nature of both the cheese and the wine. Blanket statements about cheese and wine being good companions refer to everyday or indifferent wines. Certainly if a wine has negative qualities, these will be masked by cheese, especially a strong-flavored one. By the same token, a powerful cheese will overwhelm the exquisite subtleties of a fine wine.

That said, there are many magical partnerships that are very easy to get right, particularly if you are looking for a match for a decent red wine–perhaps one that has been carried over from the main course. In this case, you could choose from the many hard and semi-hard cheeses, such as Gruyère, Beaufort, Comté, Emmenthal, Appenzel, mild Cheddar, Cheshire, and fontina, to name a few. You might also pick your way carefully around the semi-soft and soft cheeses. Among the soft fermented cheeses, Reblochon and Pont l'Évêque are probably the best bet, but only if they have been well cared for and remain delicate–almost sweet–in flavor. Be very cautious if you want to include Camembert and Brie; when ripe, these cheeses can acquire an acrid taste of ammonia that will kill good wine. It is best not to buy them too far in advance because they deteriorate rapidly after a day or two.

If you are serving a Sancerre or Pouilly Fumé with the main course and suspect it will be carried over to the cheese course, then you have the opportunity to enjoy one of the world's most sublime cheese and wine alliances, that of white goat cheese and flinty white wine. With a selection of at least six goat cheeses, you can create a cheeseboard that is virtually very exciting, particularly if you line the board, or a large flat-bottomed basket, with glossy green grape leaves, or plane tree or chestnut leaves.

One of the great challenges of the cheeseboard is finding a match for strong, salty, blue cheese, whose aggressive nature has a distinctly discouraging effect on fine red wines. Roquefort, for example, despite its wondrous qualities, will completely annihilate most wines. However, most blue cheese—and Roquefort in particular—make good partners for Sauternes and other dessert wines. So you can serve Sauternes with the dessert course, then continue the wine into the cheese course.

If you don't plan to offer a dessert wine, port goes well with strong blues, especially Stilton. If you're particularly keen on having a red wine, you could try a powerful, full-bodied one such as Zinfandel or, for special occasions, Gigondas or Côte Rotie.

A young-to-middle-aged Gorgonzola or Bresse Bleu, or a milder blue such as dolcelatte or dolcelatte torta, is a good match for a Zinfandel, Barolo, or Barbaresco. A well-aged Gorgonzola, however, would probably be too challenging in its pungency and sharpness even for such robust wines.

Cooking with Cheese

All cheeses have unique characteristics, but there are a few points to bear in mind when deciding which to cook with. Generally I find I use fresh cheeses more in summer for light dishes and desserts and in winter harder cheeses, which add warmth and depth of flavor. Hard cheeses such as Parmesan, Cheddar, and Gruyère are the most popular for cooking. Their good melting qualities make them ideal for sauces, pasta, and gratins. Blue cheeses lend real depth of flavor to dishes, and pungent ones such as Roquefort should be added sparingly. Soft rinded cheeses such as Brie and Camembert types are not often used in cooking because their large proportion of rind makes them wasteful. However, they are delicious melted on top of soups or bread and can also be broiled or baked whole. Goat cheeses are increasingly popular and are very versatile—try them in salads, pizzas, sauces, stuffings, and even desserts.

Cheese reacts differently depending on how it is cooked. The main principle is that it should not be exposed to too fierce a heat—except when broiling, in which case the cooking time should be brief. Overcooked cheese tends to be rubbery. Above a certain temperature the protein coagulates, separating the fat and water to produce a stringy texture. The secret is to add the cheese toward the end of cooking. If you are using it in a sauce, always take the pan off the heat and allow the cheese to melt in.

Hard cheeses can withstand higher temperatures than soft ones. Varieties such as haloumi, feta, and mozzarella are best cooked quickly at a high temperature. The classic example is mozzarella cooked in the blazing heat of a traditional pizza oven. The high fat or water content of soft cheeses means they blend easily with liquid, making them useful for vinaigrettes and other

uncooked sauces (see the recipe for Goat Cheese and Cumin Vinaigrette on page 20).

Finally, a couple of tips: When grating cheese, chill it first to firm it up as this makes the job easier. And take care when seasoning cheese dishes as most cheeses contain added salt—taste first.

Cheese and Your Health

Cheese can make a valuable contribution to our diet, supplying generous amounts of protein, vitamin A, and calcium, which helps prevent osteoporosis. It also contains vitamins B2, B12 and D, niacin, and folic acid, as well as phosphorus and zinc. It is beneficial to children, because calcium aids the growth of strong bones and teeth, and also to the elderly, because it provides a concentration of nutrients the might otherwise be lacking in their diet. The vitamin B12 is especially welcome for vegetarians, who may like to seek out cheeses made with a vegetarian rennet substitute rather than traditional rennet—a substance extracted from the stomach lining of calves to clot the milk.

There's no denying, however, that many cheeses are high in fat—a cause of dietary concern for most of us nowadays. But I down believe it's possible to enjoy cheese as part of a healthy diet. As in all things, moderation is the key. Set out to discover the wealth of artisan cheeses on offer and enjoy them just two or three times a week. This is more satisfying than consuming bland, plastic-wrapped, factory-produced cheeses on a daily basis. A lump of good farmhouse cheese, a hunk of bread, and some salad make for a fulfilling meal, and you won't need butter or any other form of fat with it.

In cooking, it really pays to use good-quality cheeses. If you add a farmhouse Cheddar to your cheese sauce rather than a factory one, for example, you will find the taste is so much stronger that you can get away with using less. The farmhouse version may be more expensive, but you will save on both calories and cost.

Soft ripened cheeses such as Brie and Camembert are not as calorific as you might think, containing around two-thirds the fat of hard cheeses such as Cheddar and only half the fat of Stilton. And, of course, there are cheeses that are naturally low-fat, mainly the soft ones such as ricotta, fromage frais, cottage cheese, and quark. You will find recipes for all of these in this book. But please, don't use half-fat cheeses on sale in some supermarkets. These may have only half the fat, but they have absolutely none of the flavor.

Several years ago, an irrational fear developed in Britain about the health risks of unpasteurized cheeses, which were wrongly seen as causing listeriosis. Since then, the government's Chief Medical Officer has completely exonerated unpasteurized cheeses, and mercifully, they are just as safe to eat as pasteurized ones. However, there is a slight risk of listeriosis from rinded and mold-ripened cheeses (e.g. Camembert and Stilton), whether pasteurized or unpasteurized. Current advice is that these should be avoided by pregnant women, the very young, the very old, and anyone suffering from an immune-deficiency illness.

Cheese	Carbohydrates (g)	Fat (g)	Protein (g)	Calories (Kcal)
Brie	Trace	26.9	19.3	319
Camembert	Trace	23.7	20.9	297
Chaumes	1.0	25.4	21.0	317
Cheddar	0.1	34.4	25.5	410
Chèvre	Trace	25.6	21.0	314
Danish Blue	0.1	29.0	20.0	336
Dolcelatte	Trace	36.0	17.3	394
Edam	Trace	24.1	27.1	326
Feta	3.0	24.2	17.2	298
Fontina	0.1	30.45	25.2	381
Gorgonzola	Trace	26.0	19.0	333
Gouda	Trace	31.0	24.0	375
Gruyère	0.8	32.0	28.0	403
Mascarpone	4.8	40.30	5.5	404
Mozzarella (full-fat)	Trace	25.4	18.0	301
Mozzarella (half-fat)	1.8	10.5	20.0	182
Parmesan	Trace	32.7	39.4	452
Pont L'Évêque	Trace	22.5	24.0	299
Ricotta (full-fat)	2.6	14.8	10.0	185
Roquefort	1.8	29.0	21.0	352
Stilton	0.1	35.5	22.7	411

Notes on the Recipes

- Butter is always unsalted.
- Eggs are extra large free-range.
- In white sauces, boiled milk is often specified. Although this is not essential, bringing the milk to a boil and then straining it before adding it to the sauce gives a smoother finish.
- Alternative cheeses are suggested in most recipes. These are recommended replacements if the cheese in the ingredients list is hard to find.

Occasionally, though, I have suggested a completely different cheese. This is to give a new twist to the existing recipe–for example, replacing the Cheddar in a soup with goat cheese or Stilton. Feel free to experiment.

IMPORTANT

Some of the recipes contain raw or lightly cooked eggs, which may carry a slight risk of salmonella poisoning. These should be avoided by the very young, the very old, anyone suffering from an immune-deficiency illness, and pregnant women.

Because of the marginal risk of listeriosis, it is also advisable that these groups steer clear of rinded and mold-ripened cheeses.

BASICS

Vegetable Stock

MAKES about 1 quart

2 tablespoons olive oil
1 onion chopped
1 small leek, chopped
½ cup chopped celery root
2 large carrots, chopped
1 celery stalk, chopped
¾ cup chopped white cabbage
½ bulb fennel, chopped
4 garlic cloves, chopped
½ cup white wine (optional)
4 black peppercorns
1 sprig of fresh thyme
1 bay leaf
1½ quarts water
2 teaspoons salt

There are as many different recipes for vegetable stock as there are cooks, but most of them contain sweet-tasting vegetables such as carrots and leeks.

Heat the oil in a large pot, add all the vegetables and the garlic, and cook gently for about 5 minutes, until softened. Add the wine, if using, then add the peppercorns, thyme, bay leaf, and water.

Bring to the boil. Add the salt and simmer for 40 minutes, until reduced by a third of its original volume. Strain through a fine sieve and leave to cool. Refrigerate until required or freeze.

P.G.TIPS **You can buy canned bouillon in supermarkets. These are generally of good quality and can be used in all the recipes requiring stock in this book. However, some of them are quite salty, so be careful when adding seasoning. Homemade stocks are, of course, considerably cheaper.**

Chicken Stock

MAKES about 7 ½ cups

5 pounds raw chicken carcasses, or chicken wings & legs
2½ cups chopped onions
1½ cups chopped carrots
1¼ cups chopped celery
1 leek, chopped
1 bouquet garni (see Tip)

A light, clear, refined chicken stock, ideal for sauces and soups.

Put the chicken carcasses in a large pot, cover with cold water, and bring slowly to a boil. Skim off any impurities that rise to the surface, then add the vegetables and bouquet garni. Simmer very gently for 4 hours, then strain through a fine sieve and leave to cool. Refrigerate the stock until it is required or freeze.

 P.G.TIPS **To make a bouquet garni, tie together 1 bay leaf and 2 sprigs each of fresh parsley and thyme and wrap in a small strip of green of leek.**

Cheese-Infused Chicken Stock

MAKES about 1 quart

1 tablespoon unsalted butter
1 onion, sliced
1 leek, sliced
2 garlic cloves, halved
1 quart Chicken Stock (see opposite)
A few sprigs each of fresh parsley, rosemary & thyme
½ cup rinds of hard cheese

This is ideal for using those last pieces of cheese and rind that are left after grating as much as you can from a piece. Parmesan is perfect for this recipe. The cheese adds a wonderfully rich flavor to the stock, which can be used as a base for risottos, pastas, sauces, and soups.

Heat the butter in a heavy-based pot. Add the onion, leek, and garlic and cook over a gentle heat until softened. Add the chicken stock, herbs, and cheese rind and bring to a boil.

Reduce the heat and simmer for 20 minutes, then strain through a fine sieve and leave to cool. Refrigerate the stock until it is required or freeze.

Meat Stock

MAKES about 7 ½ cups

6 tablespoons vegetable oil
2 pounds beef or veal bones, chopped into small pieces
1 pound beef or veal trimmings, cut into small pieces
3 carrots, chopped
2 onions, chopped
1 celery stalk, chopped
2 garlic cloves, smashed
¼ cup tomato paste
1 bouquet garni (see Tip opposite)

You can use beef or veal bones to make this, but veal give a better flavor.

Preheat the oven to 425°F. Heat half the oil in a roasting pan, add the bones, and roast them for about 30 minutes, until well browned. Meanwhile, heat the remaining oil in a large pot and fry the meat trimmings until very well browned.

Add the bones, vegetables, and garlic to the pot, cover with water, and bring slowly to a boil. Skim off any impurities that rise to the surface. Stir in the tomato paste and bouquet garni and simmer over a very low heat for 2 hours, skimming frequently. Strain through a fine sieve and leave to cool. Refrigerate until required or freeze.

Reduced Meat Stock

Pour the strained meat stock into a pan and boil until reduced by half its volume. Store or freeze as above

Basic Cheese Sauce (Sauce Mornay)

MAKES about 2½ cups

3¾ cups milk

1 onion, peeled & studded with 3-4 cloves

4 tablespoons unsalted butter

⅓ cup all-purpose flour

1 cup grated Gruyère cheese

1 teaspoon Dijon mustard

Freshly grated nutmeg

Salt & freshly ground black pepper

½ cup heavy cream

2 egg yolks

ALTERNATIVE CHEESES

For an interestingly different sauce, replace the Gruyère with a goat cheese or blue cheese

This is a classic white sauce that has been enriched with cream and egg and includes Gruyère cheese.

Put the milk and onion in a pan and bring to a boil, then remove from the heat and let stand for 5 minutes. Melt the butter in a separate pan and stir in the flour to make a *roux*. Cook gently, stirring, for 2-3 minutes.

Remove the onion from the milk and add the milk to the *roux* a little at a time, stirring constantly. Bring slowly to a boil, then reduce the heat and cook very gently for 20 minutes, stirring from time to time to prevent sticking.

Remove from the heat, add the cheese, and stir until melted. Add the mustard and season with nutmeg, salt, and pepper. If you like, strain through a fine sieve for a smoother sauce. Stir in the cream and egg yolks.

Rapid Cheese Sauce

SERVES 4

½ cup Vegetable Stock (see page 16)

½ cup heavy cream

6 tablespoons freshly grated Parmesan cheese

2 teaspoons arrowroot

6 tablespoons chilled unsalted butter, cut into small pieces

Salt & freshly ground black pepper

This sauce is simple to make and the result is both satisfying and tasty.

Bring the vegetable stock and cream to a boil and boil for 2-3 minutes. Put the cheese and arrowroot in a bowl and mix to a paste with a little water. Add to the stock and stir over a gentle heat until thickened. Whisk in the butter a few pieces at a time until smooth and creamy. Season to taste and serve immediately.

 P.G.TIPS To serve this sauce with fish, you can make it taste more interesting by adding fresh herbs such as chervil, chives, and tarragon.

Cheese Butters

SERVES 4

These can be prepared well ahead of time and stored in the refrigerator or even the freezer. You can then cut off slices to use as required—perhaps as a topping from grilled fish, steak, or vegetables.

Camembert Butter

MAKES about ³/₄ cup

¼ Camembert cheese, rind removed
9 tablespoons unsalted butter, softened
Freshly ground black pepper

Process all the ingredients together in a blender or food processor, then scrape out onto a piece of foil. Shape into a log and roll up in the foil, then chill until required.

Roquefort Butter

MAKES 1 heaped cup

4 ounces Roquefort cheese
10 tablespoons unsalted butter, softened
1 tablespoon chopped fresh parsley
Freshly ground black pepper

Prepare as for Camembert Butter.

Roquefort & Green Peppercorn Butter

Stir 1 tablespoon crushed green peppercorns into the Roquefort Butter.

Ricotta, Thyme & Garlic Butter

MAKES 1 cup

½ cup ricotta cheese
½ cup (1 stick) unsalted butter, softened
1 garlic clove, minced
1 tablespoon fresh lemon thyme leaves

Prepare as for Camembert Butter.

Cilantro & Goat Cheese Pesto

MAKES about 1¼ cups

1 garlic clove, minced

1 cup fresh cilantro leaves

1 tablespoon pine nuts

⅔ cup extra-virgin olive oil

2 tablespoons freshly grated Parmesan cheese

3 ounces (about scant ½ cup) soft mild goat cheese, such as Sainte-Maure, Golden Cross, Roubiliac or Montrachet

¼ cup mascarpone cheese

Salt & freshly ground black pepper

ALTERNATIVE
CHEESES

Kervella (Australia) or any other soft goat cheese

Throughout this book you will discover the versatility of this sauce. It is wonderful with fresh pasta, and can also be used as a stuffing for vegetables, fish, or chicken if you halve the amount of olive oil. You could also vary the herbs, replacing the cilantro with basil, for example, or with a combination of fresh herbs.

Put the garlic, cilantro, and pine nuts in a blender and blitz to a purée, gradually adding the olive oil. Add the cheeses and blend again until the mixture has a thick, saucelike consistency. Season with salt and pepper.

Goat Cheese & Cumin Vinaigrette

MAKES about 1¼ cups

4 ounces (about ½ cup) soft mild goat cheese such as Golden Cross, or Montrachet

2 tablespoons hot water

2 tablespoons red wine vinegar

½ tablespoon ground cumin

1 tablespoon chopped fresh oregano (optional)

1 egg yolk

7 tablespoons vegetable oil or peanut oil

Salt & freshly ground black pepper

This unusual vinaigrette can be served with spring vegetable salads and is also delicious with Carpaccio of Beef (see page 48) as an alternative to the dolcelatte mustard dressing.

Put the goat cheese in a bowl, pour on the hot water, and beat until smooth and creamy. Add the vinegar, cumin, oregano, if using, and egg yolk and whisk together until blended. Gradually whisk in the oil and then season to taste, being careful with the amount of salt you add as some goat cheeses have a rather salty flavor.

Quark Mayonnaise

SERVES 4

2 egg yolks
2 tablespoons red wine vinegar
Salt & freshly ground black pepper
¼ cup olive oil
1 cup low-fat quark
2 tablespoons water

ALTERNATIVE

CHEESES

Low-fat fromage blanc, ricotta, or
farmer's cheese

Quark is extremely low in fat and so is very useful for anyone trying to reduce their fat intake—for whom mayonnaise would usually be out of bounds because of all the oil it contains. Although this recipe includes a little olive oil for flavor, most of it is replaced by quark, resulting in an altogether healthier mayonnaise with a smooth consistency and delicate flavor.

Whisk the egg yolks and vinegar with a pinch of salt until creamy. Whisk in the oil a little at a time, as if making mayonnaise, to form a light emulsion. Blend the quark with the water and add to the egg mixture, then season to taste with salt and pepper.

Basic Pie Pastry

MAKES 1 pound

1⅔ cups all-purpose flour
¾ cup (1½ sticks) chilled, unsalted butter,
cut into small pieces
1 egg, beaten
A pinch of salt

To make cheese pastry, add ¼ cup freshly grated Parmesan to the flour with the butter.

Sift the flour onto a work surface or into a large bowl. Add the butter and blend together with your fingertips until it has a soft, Sandy texture. Make well in the center and add the beaten egg and salt. Gently mix together with your fingertips to form a smooth, even dough. Wrap in plastic wrap and chill for about 30 minutes or until required.

Sweet Pastry

MAKES 1½ pounds

2⅓ cups all-purpose flour
1 cup (2 sticks) unsalted butter, cut into
small pieces (at room temperature)
A pinch of salt
1 cup confectioners' sugar, sifted
Finely grated zest of ½ lemon
1 egg, beaten

This rich pastry is suitable for most sweet tarts.

Sift the flour onto a work surface and make a well in the center. Put the butter, salt, sugar, and lemon zest in the well and then add the egg. With your fingertips, gradually bring the flour into the center until all the ingredients come together to form a soft dough. Knead very lightly for 1 minute, until completely smooth, then form the dough into a ball. Wrap in plastic wrap and chill for 2 hours.

Brioche

MAKES 12 buns or 1 loaf

1 cake (0.6 ounce) compressed fresh yeast

2 tablespoons milk

4 cups all-purpose flour

1 teaspoon salt

1½ tablespoons sugar

4 eggs

½ cup (1 stick) unsalted butter, softened

1 egg beaten with 1 tablespoon of milk, to glaze

This quick and easy brioche is great for breakfast, but can also be used in both savory and sweet dishes, such as Warm Brioche of Goat Cheese with Minted Leeks (see page 40) and Croque Mademoiselle (see page 178).

Dissolve the yeast in the milk. Sift the flour, salt, and sugar onto a work surface and make a well in the center. Beat the eggs with the yeast mixture, then pour into the well in the flour. Gradually work the flour into the eggs with the heel of your hand until a soft dough is formed, then knead it for 2-3 minutes. Work in the softened butter, using the same method, and knead for about 10 minutes or until the dough has a smooth texture. It will feel slightly sticky to the touch. Cover with plastic wrap and let rest in the refrigerator for 30 minutes.

Shape the dough into 12 balls and place in buttered individual brioche molds. Or shape it into a loaf and place in a loaf pan. Cover and let rise in a warm place for 30-40 minutes, until doubled in size. Preheat the oven to 400°F.

Brush the brioche with the beaten egg and milk mixture and bake until golden brown–about 20 minutes for brioche buns, 40 minutes for a loaf. Turn out onto a wire rack to cool.

Cheddar & Onion Loaf

MAKES 1 loaf

1 heaped teaspoon compressed fresh yeast

½ cup water

2 teaspoons vegetable oil

2½ cups all-purpose flour

A pinch of salt

A pinch of sugar

1 egg, beaten

¼ cup finely diced onion

1½ cups grated aged farmhouse Cheddar cheese

¼ cup freshly grated Parmesan cheese

This loaf (see photograph on page 189) is very quick as it needs only one rising. Although most recipes tell you to use warm water when making bread, I find cold water works perfectly well. In fact, it is probably safer, since if the water is too hot is may kill the yeast and prevent the loaf rising.

Put the yeast in a small bowl, add the water, and stir until the yeast has dissolved. Stir in the oil. Sift the flour, salt, and sugar into a bowl and make a well in the center. Pour in the yeast liquid and half the beaten egg and then stir in the flour to make a soft dough. Turn out onto a lightly floured work surface and knead for 8-10 minutes, until smooth and elastic. Let relax for 2-3 minutes, then work in the diced onion and grated cheeses. Knead for about 2 minutes, until they are fully incorporated. Shape the dough into a loaf and place it in a greased 8½- by 4½- by 2½ inch loaf pan. Cover with a damp dish towel and let rise in a warm place for about 1 hour, until doubled in size.

Preheat the oven to 425°F. Brush the top of the loaf with the remaining beaten egg and bake for 25-30 minutes, until the bread is golden brown and sounds hollow when turned out of the pan and tapped on the base. Turn out onto a wire rack to cool.

Stilton Bread

MAKES 2 loaves

1½ cakes (0.6 ounces) compressed fresh yeast

1¼ cups water

2 teaspoons malt extract

2 teaspoons golden syrup or light corn syrup

4½ cups all-purpose flour

2 teaspoons salt

5 ounces Stilton cheese, crumbled (about 1 heaped cup)

This is an excellent way of using up tiny bits of crumbled Stilton or other blue cheeses. Colston Bassett Stilton is a true jewel in Britain's cheesemaking revival. It may seem extravagant to use it in bread, but as the flavor is strong you don't need very much. (See the photograph on page 189).

Put the yeast in a small bowl, add a little of the water, and stir to dissolve. Stir in the malt extract and golden syrup. Sift the flour and salt into a bowl and make a well in the center. Pour in the yeast and the remaining water and then stir in the flour to make a soft dough. Turn out onto a lightly floured work surface and knead for 8-10 minutes, until smooth and elastic. Return to the cleaned bowl, cover with a damp dish towel, and let rise in a warm place for about 50 minutes, until doubled in size.

Punch down the dough and divide it in half. Roll out each piece into a rectangle about 8 by 12 inches. Sprinkle the Stilton evenly over the dough and roll up tightly. Place in 2 greased 8½- by 4½- by 2½-inch loaf pans, or shape into rounds and place on greased baking sheets. Cover with a damp dish towel and leave in a warm place, until risen. Preheat the oven to 400°F.

Sprinkle the loaves with a little flour and bake for 35-40 minutes, until the bread is golden brown on top and sounds hollow when turned out of the pan and tapped on the base. Turn out onto a wire rack to cool.

Italian Picnic Loaf

MAKES 1 loaf

1 tablespoon olive oil

2 garlic cloves, minced

1 cup drained & finely chopped sun-dried tomatoes in oil

2 tablespoons chopped black olives

1 quantity of Brioche dough (see opposite)

1 ball of cow's milk mozzarella cheese, well drained & cut into slices ¼ inch thick

Butter, for greasing

1 tablespoon freshly grated Parmesan cheese

A little milk, for brushing

Brioche dough is spread with mozzarella, olives, and sun-dried tomatoes and then rolled up, producing an attractive and colorful spiral pattern with the loaf is sliced. It's a wonderful bread to take on picnics, fresh from the oven.

Heat half the olive oil in a small pan, add the garlic, and cook gently for about 1 minute, until softened but not browned. Stir in the sun-dried tomatoes and olives and cook for 1 minute longer, then let cool.

Roll out the brioche dough into a 10-inch square. Brush with the remaining olive oil, then arrange the mozzarella in overlapping slices over the top, starting 2 inches from the edge of the dough. Sprinkle over the olive and tomato mixture, then roll up the brioche tightly like a jelly roll.

Lightly butter a 9- by 5- by 3-inch loaf pan and dust it with the grated Parmesan. Put the brioche roll in the pan, cover with a damp dish towel, and leave in a warm place for 25 minutes, until risen and puffy. Preheat the oven to 400°F.

Brush the loaf with a little milk and then bake for 25 minutes, until it is golden brown on top and sounds hollow when turned out of the pan and tapped on the base. Serve warm.

Chapter One

FIRST COURSES

Taramasalata with Cream Cheese on Tapenade Crostini

SERVES 4

3 slices of white bread, crusts removed

1 garlic clove, minced

4 ounces *tarama* (salted, dried gray mullet roe) or smoked cod's roe, skinned

6 tablespoons cream cheese

3 tablespoons lemon juice

6 tablespoons olive oil

Salt & freshly ground black pepper

2 tablespoons tapenade

8 slices of crusty French bread, about ½ inch thick

My inclusion of cream cheese in this traditional Greek smoked fish purée would doubtless bring tears to the eyes of locals. I find it mellows and rounds the smoky flavor of the roe—try it and see what you think.

Soak the white bread in a little water, or, better still, milk, for 5 minutes. Squeeze out the excess moisture, then place the bread in a blender or food processor. Add the garlic, roe, and cream cheese and blitz to a smooth purée. Add the lemon juice and 4 tablespoons of the olive oil and blend again, then transfer to a bowl. Season to taste, then chill for at least 2 hours.

To serve, mix the tapenade with the remaining olive oil. Toast the French bread, spread it with the taramasalata, and drizzle over the tapenade.

P.G. TIPS Jars of tapenade, a black olive and anchovy paste, are readily available in supermarkets and specialty food shops and the quality is usually quite good. Green olive tapenade works just as well. I like to serve these crostini with pre-dinner drinks or with a tipple of Ouzo. And why not?

Twice-Roasted Red Peppers with Feta, Capers & Olives

SERVES 4

4 large red sweet peppers
¼ cup olive oil
Salt & freshly ground black pepper
2 garlic cloves, thinly sliced
2 tablespoons chopped fresh flat-leaf parsley
12 black olives, pitted & halved
2 tablespoons capers, rinsed & drained
8 slices of feta cheese, cut ½ inch thick

For the dressing
2 tablespoons white wine vinegar
½ cup olive oil
¼ teaspoon Dijon mustard
½ small hot red chili pepper, seeded and minced

The vibrant colors of this dish are almost as enticing as its robust flavors. Although I usually serve it warm, it is also very good cold. Substitute oregano or basil for the parsley, if you like.

Preheat the oven to 400°F. Cut the peppers in half lengthwise, brush with a little of the olive oil, and season with salt and pepper. Bake for 1 hour or until tender. Remove from the oven and leave until cool enough to handle, then peel off the skin and cut the peppers lengthwise into strips ¾ inch wide.

Lightly brush a gratin dish with olive oil. Put the pepper strips in it, sprinkle with the garlic, parsley, olives, and capers, and season with salt and pepper. Lay the feta cheese slices on top and drizzle over the remaining olive oil. Bake for 10–12 minutes, until the cheese is just starting to melt.

Meanwhile, whisk together all the ingredients for the dressing and season to taste. Remove the peppers from the oven and drizzle the dressing over. Serve warm, with herb-grilled crusty bread (see Tip below).

 P.G. TIPS To make herb-grilled crusty bread, brush slices of baguette with olive oil and sprinkle with chopped fresh herbs, then toast under the broiler until golden.

Feta & Roasted Pepper Mousse with Arugula & Pine Nuts

SERVES 4

1 large red sweet pepper

⅔ cup olive oil

8 ounces Greek feta cheese

1 cup strained plain yogurt

1 garlic clove, minced

3 gelatin leaves

Salt & freshly ground black pepper

1 tablespoon balsamic vinegar

A handful of young arugula leaves

1 tablespoon pine nuts

This is my version of the Greek dish ktipiti, *which is usually a dip rather than a mousse. The saltiness of the feta cheese contrasts well with the peppery arugula.*

Preheat the oven to 400°F. Rub the pepper with 2 tablespoons of the olive oil, place on a baking sheet, and bake for 40 minutes or until tender. Leave until cool enough to handle, then peel off the skin. Cut the pepper in half and remove the seeds. Put the pepper in a blender with the feta, yogurt, garlic, and 4 tablespoons of the olive oil and blitz to a fine purée.

Put the gelatin in a small pan, cover with about 3 tablespoons of water, and leave for 5 minutes to soften. Melt over a gentle heat until clear. Stir it thoroughly into the purée and strain the mixture through a fine sieve. Season to taste. Pour into 4 ramekin dishes or coffee cups. Chill for 1–2 hours, to set.

Whisk together the balsamic vinegar and the remaining olive oil to make a dressing and season to taste with salt and pepper. Unmold the mousses onto individual serving plates. Toss the arugula leaves and pine nuts with the dressing and arrange them around the mousses.

Emmenthal Corniottes with Marc de Bourgogne

MAKES ABOUT 20

1 heaped cup fromage blanc or cream cheese

⅔ cup crème fraîche

2 tablespoons Marc de Bourgogne

1¾ cups grated Emmenthal cheese

2 eggs, beaten

Freshly grated nutmeg

Salt & freshly ground black pepper

1 quantity of basic pie pastry (see page 21)

1 egg beaten with 2 tablespoons milk, to glaze

ALTERNATIVE

CHEESES

Swiss Appenzell or Gruyère

Corniottes are little triangular pastries that can be filled with sweet or savory ingredients. Baked until crisp, they are a specialty of Burgundy, where they are served as a snack. If you don't have any Marc de Bourgogne, you could use kirsch instead.

Put the fromage blanc or cream cheese, crème fraîche, and Marc de Bourgogne in a bowl and beat in the grated Emmenthal and eggs to form a paste. Season with nutmeg, salt, and pepper and set aside.

Roll out the pastry until it is ⅛ inch thick and cut out 4-inch rounds—you should have about 20. Put some filling in the center of each one. Brush the edges with a little cold water and then pull 3 sides of the pastry up over the filling to form a point. Pinch together firmly to seal. Chill for up to 1 hour.

Preheat the oven to 400°F. Brush the pastries with the beaten egg and milk mixture and bake for 20–25 minutes, until golden. Serve hot or warm.

P.G.TIPS Smaller *corniottes* make great cocktail canapés. They also freeze successfully, so they can be prepared in advance and baked straight from the freezer when required. Puff pastry works just as well as this pie pastry.

Pressed Leek Terrine with St. Agur & Green Peppercorns

SERVES 8–10

30 young leeks
A pinch of sugar
Salt & freshly ground black pepper
2 cups crumbled St. Agur cheese
2 tablespoons green peppercorns
2 hard-boiled eggs, whites & yolks
  separated & chopped
2 shallots, minced
1 tablespoon chopped fresh tarragon

For the dressing
2 tablespoons champagne vinegar
½ cup walnut oil
½ teaspoon Dijon mustard

ALTERNATIVE
CHEESES

Any type of blue cheese is suitable.
Try Bleu des Causses or Roquefort.

I suggest you make this terrine for a special occasion, as it takes a little while to prepare. It should not be kept for long, otherwise its freshness and crispness will be lost.

Trim the leeks, wash them well, and cut them into 8 to 10 inch lengths. Bring a large pan of water to a boil with the sugar and some salt. Throw in the leeks, return to a boil, and cook for 8–10 minutes, until just tender. Remove the leeks and cool slightly. Squeeze out all excess moisture and dry them in a cloth.

Line an 8½- by 4½- × 2½-inch loaf pan with plastic wrap, leaving a 2-inch overhang on all sides. Cover the bottom with a layer of about 6–8 leeks (or more if needed), with the white parts at one end, and season with salt and pepper. Sprinkle over some of the cheese, peppercorns, white and yolk of egg, shallots, and tarragon. Lay more leeks on top; the green tops should rest on the white part of the previous layer. Scatter with the filling ingredients as before. Continue layering in this way, seasoning throughout, until the loaf pan is full. Finish with a layer of leeks. Fold over the plastic wrap to cover the leeks.

Place a board that will just fit inside the pan on top of the leeks, and put a heavy weight (such as a couple of cans of food) on top of that to press the filling. Refrigerate overnight.

To serve, unmold the terrine and peel off the plastic wrap. Using a sharp, long-bladed knife (or better still, an electric knife), cut the terrine into slices about ½ inch thick and place on individual serving plates. Whisk together the ingredients for the dressing, season with salt and pepper, and drizzle it around the slices of terrine.

Glazed Oysters on Crushed Potatoes with Parsley & Maytag Blue

SERVES 4
....

8–9 ounces new potatoes
¼ cup milk
¼ cup olive oil
2 tablespoons chopped fresh flat-leaf parsley
Salt & freshly ground black pepper
24 plump oysters

For the sauce
2 egg yolks
¼ cup dry white wine
⅔ cup heavy cream
½ cup crumbled Maytag Blue cheese

ALTERNATIVE
....
CHEESES
....

Roquefort or Oregon Blue

The combination of oysters and blue cheese may sound unexpected, but it is a marriage made in culinary heaven. This is my version of a dish I came across at the Bel-Air Hotel in Los Angeles, during a week I spent there as guest chef. Maytag Blue, a creamy, salty cheese from Iowa, is perfect for this preparation.

Cook the potatoes in boiling salted water until just tender, then drain well. Place in a bowl, add the milk, olive oil, and parsley and crush them coarsely with a fork. Season with salt and pepper and keep warm.

Open the oysters and remove from the shells, reserving the juices (see Tip below). Discard the top part of each shell and clean the bottom part.

For the sauce, whisk the egg yolks and wine together in a small bowl or the top of a double boiler. Set the bowl over a pan of simmering water and whisk until the mixture thickens and doubles in volume. Boil the cream and cheese together for 2–3 minutes, then fold into the whisked egg yolk and wine mixture along with the strained oyster juices.

To serve, divide the crushed potatoes between the cleaned oyster shells. Season the oysters, put them on top of the potato mixture, and coat with the sauce. Place under the broiler for 5 minutes, until golden (or place in a hot oven). Serve immediately.

P.G.TIPS To open oysters you need an oyster knife or other short, strong-bladed knife. Wrap your hand in a dish towel to protect it, then take hold of an oyster and insert the knife blade between the shells, next to the hinge. Twist the knife to lever open the top shell, then cut the muscle connecting the oyster to the shell. Next, loosen the muscle connecting the oyster to the bottom shell. Take out the oyster and strain the juices into a bowl.

GLAZED OYSTERS ON
CRUSHED POTATOES WITH
PARSLEY & MAYTAG BLUE

Parmesan Brioche Toast with Taleggio, Sautéed Plum Tomatoes & Oregano

SERVES 4

2 tablespoons olive oil

2 garlic cloves, minced

1 pound small plum tomatoes, halved

Salt & freshly ground black pepper

2 tablespoons chopped fresh oregano

2 eggs, beaten

½ cup milk

½ cup freshly grated Parmesan cheese

Freshly grated nutmeg

4 slices of brioche (see page 22), cut
¾ inch thick

3 tablespoons unsalted butter

½ cup aged Taleggio cheese slivers

ALTERNATIVE
CHEESES

Substitute freshly shaved Parmesan or
Asiago for the Taleggio

This simple recipe is a savory version of French toast. A good aged Taleggio cheese adds a creamy, aromatic, and slightly sour flavor, which partners the sweetness of the tomatoes and brioche well. If yellow plum tomatoes are available, why not use half red, half yellow? The colors look stunning.

Heat the oil in a pan, add the garlic, and cook for 1 minute. Add the tomatoes and sauté them until they begin to soften. Season with salt and pepper and stir in the oregano. Keep warm.

In a shallow bowl, whisk together the eggs, milk, and Parmesan cheese, seasoning with a little nutmeg, salt, and pepper. Cut the brioche slices into rounds, if desired, or leave them whole. Dip them in the egg mixture on both sides. Heat the butter in a frying pan, add the brioche, and cook for 2–3 minutes on each side, until golden.

Put the Parmesan French toasts on serving plates and arrange the tomatoes on top. Scatter over the Taleggio and place under the broiler to melt the cheese slightly before serving.

P.G.TIPS   It's important to use good, sweet, ripe tomatoes here. Plum tomatoes are generally fuller flavored, but if they are not readily available, try using the larger, rounded varieties, sliced. Add a pinch of sugar if their flavor is not all it should be. English muffins can be substituted for the brioche.

PARMESAN BRIOCHE TOAST WITH
TALEGGIO, SAUTÉED PLUM TOMATOES
& OREGANO

Ratatouille-Stuffed Mozzarella Wrapped in Prosciutto

SERVES 4

3 tablespoons extra-virgin olive oil
1 small eggplant, sliced
1 zucchini, sliced
1 garlic clove, minced
1 teaspoon chopped fresh thyme
Salt & freshly ground black pepper
2 balls of cow's milk mozzarella cheese
2 plum tomatoes, skinned & sliced
8 thin slices of prosciutto
4 tablespoons unsalted butter

For the dressing
2 tablespoons balsamic vinegar
6 tablespoons extra-virgin olive oil
1 tomato, skinned, seeded & diced
½ tablespoon chopped black olives
6 fresh basil leaves, shredded

ALTERNATIVE

CHEESE

Provolone

Although buffalo mozzarella is generally held to be superior to cow's milk mozzarella, in this recipe I actually prefer to use the cow's milk cheese because it is less milky in texture and holds its shape better.

To make the ratatouille, heat the oil in a frying pan and fry the eggplant and zucchini slices until tender. Stir in the garlic and thyme and cook for 1 minute, then season and let cool.

Cut each mozzarella horizontally into 4 equal slices and season lightly. Cover 4 slices with layers of eggplant, zucchini and tomato, then top with the remaining cheese slices, making 4 ratatouille-stuffed mozzarella sandwiches in all. Wrap each one in 2 slices of prosciutto to secure the filling and chill for at least 30 minutes.

Heat the butter in a large frying pan, add the cheese sandwiches, and fry until golden, about 2–3 minutes on each side. Place on 4 serving plates. Mix together all the ingredients for the dressing and season to taste. Pour it over the cheese sandwiches and serve.

P.G.TIPS

Try grilling the stuffed mozzarella over charcoal for a superb smoky flavor. Some people may be surprised to see that I do not advise salting the eggplant in this recipe. When slicing eggplants thinly, I see little point in the exercise. However, when I use them in halves, I do usually salt them before cooking.

Roasted Eggplant Moutabel with Goat Cheese & Thyme

SERVES 4

3 medium eggplants

2 tablespoons tahini (sesame seed paste)

1 garlic clove, minced

1 teaspoon ground cumin

2 tablespoons lemon juice

Salt & freshly ground black pepper

1 goat cheese log, cut into 12 slices

2 tablespoons fresh thyme leaves

¼ cup walnut oil

ALTERNATIVE

CHEESE

Any soft fresh goat cheese log

Moutabel is a Middle Eastern dish of puréed eggplant and tahini, also known as baba ghanoush. I find eggplants have a great affinity with cheese. In this dish, eggplant halves are stuffed with a moutabel-style filling and then topped with goat cheese and thyme. It is one of my favorite combinations. Serve on some salad leaves with a dressing of Middle Eastern flavors, such as a vinaigrette containing peeled, seeded, and finely diced tomato, chopped fresh cilantro, and a little ground cumin.

Preheat the oven to 375°F. Cut the eggplants in half, score the cut sides with a knife in a criss-cross pattern, and bake for 45 minutes to 1 hour, until tender. The exterior should be slightly charred but not burnt. Remove from the oven and let cool, then scoop out the flesh without damaging the skins. Mince the flesh and mix it with the tahini, garlic, cumin, lemon juice, and some salt and pepper.

Refill the eggplant skins with this mixture (there may only be enough to fill 4 halves), retaining the original shape of the eggplants. Put them in a lightly oiled, shallow baking dish. Top each one with slices of goat cheese, sprinkle with the thyme leaves, and drizzle the walnut oil over. Return to the oven to bake for 8–10 minutes, until the cheese is golden and just beginning to melt. Cool slightly before serving.

Saganaki (Fried Sheep Cheese with Lemon)

SERVES 4

6 tablespoons unsalted butter

8 slices of kasseri or kefalotiri cheese, cut ¾ inch thick

Salt & freshly ground black pepper

Juice of 1 lemon

ALTERNATIVE

CHEESE

Haloumi

This dish of simply fried sheep's milk cheese is served as a staple in tavernas throughout the Greek islands. Its beauty lies in its simplicity. It must be one of the easiest dishes to prepare, with just three ingredients, but it is delicious—and exceedingly more-ish.

Heat the butter in a large frying pan until foaming, add the cheese slices, and fry for 1–2 minutes on each side, until golden. Season lightly with salt and pepper and then pour the lemon juice over the cheese in the pan. Serve immediately, with lots of crusty bread.

P.G.TIPS **The lemon juice nicely flavors the butter, but to add an extra dimension I occasionally like to add fresh capers and herbs. In Greece, the cheese is sometimes flamed with brandy at the table.**

Goyère

SERVES 4–6

3 cups potatoes cut into small cubes

2 tablespoons unsalted butter

1 small onion, minced

4 ounces (4 slices) bacon, chopped

4½ ounces Munster cheese, rind removed, cut in ¼ inch dice (about ½ heaped cup)

2 eggs, beaten

½ cup crème fraîche or heavy cream

Salt & freshly ground black pepper

For the base

6 tablespoons unsalted butter

3 tablespoons milk

1 cake (0.6 ounce) compressed fresh yeast

2 cups all-purpose flour

2 eggs, beaten

A pinch of salt

A pinch of brown sugar

ALTERNATIVE CHEESE

Connoisseurs should look out for an interesting English cheese called Stinking Bishop. The rind is washed with the pear variety of the same name, also used to make perry or pear cider, which gives the cheese its strong-smelling yet creamy-tasting character

Like flamiche *(see page 41), goyère is a rich cheese tart from Belgium and northern France. Some recipes specify a pastry base while others use a bread dough, similar to that of a pizza. Here I give my favorite version, which has a yeasted dough for the base. The filling for goyère is generally made with a pungent—or, frankly, smelly—rindwashed cheese such as Maroilles or Livarot. Not for the faint-hearted, but when mixed with smoked bacon and potatoes it makes a wonderfully flavored dish.*

For the base, warm the butter and milk over a low heat until the butter has just melted. Leave until tepid, then stir in the yeast until dissolved. Sift the flour into a bowl, make a well in the center, and add the beaten eggs, salt, and brown sugar. Add the yeast mixture to the eggs and mix in the flour to give a smooth dough. Turn the dough out onto a lightly floured work surface and knead for 5 minutes or until smooth. Return it to the cleaned bowl, cover with a damp cloth, and let rise in a warm place until doubled in size.

For the filling, cook the potatoes in boiling salted water until just tender, then drain well. Heat the butter in a pan, add the onion, and cook over a gentle heat until soft but not colored. Add the bacon and cook for 5 minutes, then remove from the heat and let cool.

Put the potatoes, onion, bacon, and cheese in a bowl and mix in the eggs and crème fraîche or cream. Season to taste with salt and pepper.

Punch down the risen dough and roll out until it is ¼ inch thick. Use to line a 9-inch flan ring set on a baking sheet, or a tart pan, leaving a good amount of dough hanging over the edge. Fill with the potato, bacon, and cheese mixture and let rise in a warm place for 30 minutes, until the dough is puffy. Preheat the oven to 325°F.

Trim off the excess dough, then bake the tart in the oven for 45 minutes to 1 hour, until golden and set.

Pear, Roquefort Blue & Rosemary Galettes

SERVES 4

2 medium egg whites

8–9 ounces Roquefort cheese

1 tablespoon crème fraîche

Salt & freshly ground black pepper

1 quantity of basic pie pastry (see page 21)

1 tablespoon finely chopped fresh rosemary, plus a few leaves to garnish

4 tablespoons unsalted butter, plus a little melted butter for brushing

2 large, ripe, but firm pears, peeled, cored & cut into slices ½ inch thick

1 tablespoon sugar

1 teaspoon cumin seeds

2 egg yolks, beaten with 1 tablespoon milk, to glaze

ALTERNATIVE
CHEESES

A fairly sharp blue cheese is needed, such as Gorgonzola

Ripe, sweet pears make an excellent foil for sharp blue cheese and aromatic rosemary. As an alternative dish, try replacing the pear and Roquefort with slices of mozzarella and tomato, top them with a covering of pesto, and bake the galettes as usual.

Whisk the egg whites until just frothy. Put the cheese in a bowl and crush it lightly with a fork, then add the egg whites and crème fraîche and mix to a coarse paste. Season with salt and pepper, then chill.

Roll out the pastry to about ⅛ inch thick. Using a plain or fluted round cutter, cut out four 5-inch disks. Put them on a baking sheet and prick well all over with a fork to prevent them from rising too much in the oven. Carefully spread the cheese mixture over the pastry disks, leaving a ½- to ¾-inch border. Sprinkle with the chopped rosemary and place in the refrigerator.

Preheat the oven to 400°F. Melt the butter in a shallow pan and add the pear slices, sugar, and enough water to form a light syrup around the pears—about 3 tablespoons. Cook gently for 6–8 minutes, until the pears are tender, then let cool.

Arrange the pear slices on top of the galettes in neatly overlapping circles. Brush with a little melted butter. Sprinkle with the cumin seeds and a few rosemary leaves and season with salt and pepper. Bring up the edges of the pastry over the pears to form a crust. Brush the pastry all over with the egg yolk glaze, then bake for 15–20 minutes or until golden. Cool the galettes slightly before serving.

P.G. TIPS

The galettes can be assembled several hours in advance—or even the night before—and chilled until you are ready to bake them. If you prefer, you can use puff pastry instead of basic pie pastry.

PEAR, ROQUEFORT & ROSEMARY GALETTE

Warm Brioche of Goat Cheese with Minted Leeks

SERVES 4

4 tablespoons unsalted butter

2 young leeks, thinly sliced

1 tablespoon chopped fresh mint

Freshly grated nutmeg

Salt & freshly ground black pepper

4 brioche buns, 2 inches in diameter (see page 22)

4 crottin de Chavignol goat cheeses, cut horizontally in half

ALTERNATIVE
CHEESES

A good English alternative is a well-aged Chabis, produced in East Sussex on the same farm as Golden Cross. Or you could use 4 slices of Sainte-Maure goat cheese, cut 1 inch thick

I first prepared this brioche for a private party of eight vegetarians in the Lanesborough's Conservatory restaurant, as part of a seven-course gastronomic vegetarian menu. It was voted the star of the show and now makes regular appearances on my menu.

Preheat the oven to 400°F. Melt the butter in a pan, add the leeks, and cook over a low heat for 8–10 minutes or until tender. You may need to add a little water if the leeks become too dry and stick to the pan. Remove from the pan and stir in the mint, then season to taste with nutmeg, salt, and pepper.

Cut a ½-inch slice off the top of each brioche and set aside, then carefully hollow out the center of each bun. Fill with the minted leeks. Top the leeks with the goat cheese. Put the brioches in the oven for 5 minutes to heat through. The cheese should just be starting to melt. Replace the brioche tops and serve immediately.

P.G.TIPS Try topping the cheese with a little basil pesto before putting the brioches in the oven. I much prefer to prepare fresh pesto, which can be made in minutes in a blender. Store-bought pesto is fine, but nothing quite matches the flavor and aroma of fresh basil. Phyllo pastry makes a good substitute for the brioche: Simply top the leeks with the cheese and wrap well in phyllo, then bake until golden.

Flamiche aux Trois Fromages

SERVES 4–6

3 eggs

1¼ cups heavy cream

½ cup milk

Freshly grated nutmeg

Salt & freshly ground black pepper

¾ cup Roquefort cheese, cut into ½ inch cubes

¾ cup grated Emmenthal cheese

3 ounces soft goat cheese, cut into ½-inch cubes (about ¾ cup)

9 ounces puff pastry

ALTERNATIVE
CHEESES

Any three varieties of cheese can be used, but I think a combination of goat cheese, blue cheese, and a hard cheese, strikes the perfect balance

I first had this rich cheese tart at a simple country auberge in France some ten years ago, and its intense flavors have stayed in my mind to this day. The original recipe put Sainte-Maure goat cheese with Roquefort and Emmenthal. The cheeses are added to the pastry case separately rather than mixed together, so it's rather like a mini cheeseboard in a tart! This does mean, of course, that everyone is given a slightly different slice, which is fine if your guests all have individual preferences. Otherwise, lightly stir the cheese mixtures together to give a marbled effect.

Preheat the oven to 425°F. Beat together the eggs, cream, and milk, seasoning them with nutmeg, salt, and pepper. Divide equally among 3 bowls and stir a different cheese into each one. Let stand while you prepare the pastry.

Roll out the pastry thinly and use to line a 8- to 9-inch tart pan. Prick the bottom all over with a fork to prevent it from rising too much in the oven. Carefully pour the 3 cheese mixtures into 3 separate areas of the pastry shell. Marble them lightly with a fork, if you like, or leave them separate. Bake for 30–40 minutes, until the tart is set and beautifully golden. Serve hot.

P.G.TIPS You could use basic pie pastry (see page 21) instead of puff if you prefer, but you will need to bake the pastry case unfilled for 8–10 minutes before adding the filling. For a non-traditional but luxurious addition, spread 1 cup fresh crabmeat over the bottom of the pastry shell before pouring in the filling.

Baked Reblochon in Savoy Cabbage

SERVES 4
....

3 tablespoons vegetable oil

⅔ cup potatoes cut into ¼-inch cubes

1 onion, minced

3 ounces (3 slices) bacon, cut into *lardons* (small strips)

1 cup thinly sliced chanterelle mushrooms

1½ cups thinly sliced button mushrooms

2 tablespoons chopped fresh chives

8 green cabbage leaves, such as Savoy or Primo

Freshly grated nutmeg

Salt & freshly ground black pepper

1 Reblochon cheese, rind removed

2 tablespoons unsalted butter, melted

1¼ cups Reduced Meat Stock (see page 17)

ALTERNATIVE
....
CHEESES
....

Baby Saint-Nectaire, Pont-l'Évêque, or a plain or smoked Gubbeen

I got the idea for this recipe from Pierre Carrier, the proprietor of the Hotel Albert Premier in Chamonix, France. His version used a local Reblochon made of goat's milk, which is well worth buying if you ever happen to see it. Although the dish is fairly expensive to make, the flavors are out of this world. Serve as a substantial first course or a delicious and unusual lunch dish.

Heat 1 tablespoon of the oil in a frying pan and sauté the potatoes until golden brown and just tender. Remove from the pan and set aside. Add the remaining oil to the pan and stir in the onion, bacon, and both types of mushroom. Raise the heat and cook until golden and tender. Add to the potatoes, stir in the chives, and let cool.

Preheat the oven to 400°F. Trim the cabbage leaves and cook them in boiling salted water until just tender. Remove with a slotted spoon and refresh in cold running water, then drain well and dry on a cloth. Lay out the leaves, slightly overlapping, on a work surface and season with nutmeg, salt, and pepper.

Slice the Reblochon in half horizontally. Cover one half with the potato mixture and top with the other half to form a sandwich. Place the Reblochon in the center of the cabbage leaves and fold them over to cover the cheese completely. Season again and brush with the melted butter. Place in a baking dish and bake for about 12–15 minutes, until thoroughly heated through. Meanwhile, heat the reduced meat stock. When ready, transfer the cheese to a serving dish and pour the meat stock around it. Serve cut into wedges.

P.G.TIPS Try wrapping the cheese in puff pastry rather than cabbage leaves. Swiss chard or spinach could easily replace the cabbage, if preferred. For vegetarians, the meat stock can be replaced by red wine vinegar or walnut oil dressing.

Greek-Style Baked Artichokes with Cilantro, Mint & Lemon

SERVES 4

8 medium or 4 large globe artichokes
Juice & zest of 1 lemon
1 cup fresh white bread crumbs
2 garlic cloves, minced
1 tablespoon chopped fresh mint
1 tablespoon chopped fresh cilantro
½ cup grated kasseri cheese
⅔ cup olive oil
Salt & freshly ground black pepper
¾ cup crumbled feta chese
⅔ cup dry white wine

ALTERNATIVE
CHEESES

Italian provolone

You need kasseri cheese for this recipe, a mild, creamy sheep's milk cheese which is now available from some Greek grocers. There is an American version of kasseri from Wisconsin, made with cow's milk and tasting a little sharper and saltier. The artichokes are filled with a tangy cheese and herb mixture, which also makes a very good stuffing for tomatoes and eggplants.

Preheat the oven to 350°F. To prepare the artichokes, snap off the stalks and trim away the dark, fibrous outer leaves until you reach the tender, inner green leaves, rubbing the artichokes with the lemon juice as you go to prevent discoloration. Slice off about one third from the top of each artichoke. Carefully remove the hairy inner choke with a teaspoon. Drop the artichokes into a bowl of water acidulated with lemon juice.

In a bowl, mix together the lemon zest, bread crumbs, garlic, mint, cilantro, grated kasseri, and 2 tablespoons of the olive oil. Season with salt and pepper.

Drain and dry the artichokes, then fill them with the feta. Top with the stuffing mixture. Place them in a baking dish. Sprinkle with the white wine and the remaining oil and add water until the liquid reaches halfway up the sides of the artichokes. Bake for 35 minutes or until tender, basting frequently. Put the artichokes under the broiler for a few minutes to brown the stuffing. Serve hot or cold.

GREEK-STYLE BAKED
ARTICHOKES WITH CILANTRO,
MINT & LEMON

Crisp, Flowering Zucchini with Mozzarella & Anchovy

SERVES 4

8 zucchini, about 2 inches long, with flowers still attached

4 canned anchovy fillets

1 ball of cow's milk mozzarella cheese

3 tablespoons Chinese flour (see Tip)

Vegetable oil for deep-frying

Sprigs of fresh flat-leaf parsley, to garnish

Lemon wedges, to serve

My good friend Stuart Partridge, chef at the Hassler Hotel in Rome, first prepared this dish during a recent visit to the Lanesborough. I love the pure simplicity of its flavors. You could serve the zucchini with a tomato sauce, but I like them best with just a squeeze of lemon juice. Although very young zucchini with their yellow flowers still attached are sold in markets in France and Italy, they are not as easily obtainable in the US. However, if you grow your own zucchini, or other summer squash, you can pick them for this recipe when they are just the right size.

Trim about ½ inch off the end of each zucchini and discard (or save for another use). Carefully wipe clean the zucchini flowers and remove the stamen from the center of each one. Soak the anchovy fillets in water for 10 minutes, then dry them on paper towels. Cut each anchovy fillet in half. Cut the mozzarella into 8 sticks approximately the size of your index finger. Place a piece of anchovy on each mozzarella stick, then place inside a zucchini flower and twist the end of the blossom to secure the filling.

Mix the Chinese flour with enough water to make a thin batter; it should coat the back of a spoon. Heat the oil in a deep fryer or large saucepan to 350°F. Dip the zucchini in the batter and deep-fry them for 1–2 minutes, until crisp and golden, turning them occasionally. Drain them thoroughly on paper towels. Quickly drop the sprigs of parsley into the hot oil and fry for about 10 seconds, until crisp, then drain on paper towels. Serve the zucchini immediately, garnished with the deep-fried parsley and accompanied by lemon wedges.

P.G.TIPS Chinese flour is available in Asian markets, but if you can't find any, make a tempura batter instead. Put 1 medium egg yolk and ½ cup ice water in a bowl, then gently mix in ¾ cup all-purpose flour and a pinch of salt; the batter should be slightly lumpy. Dip the zucchini in the batter and fry as above. If you are keen to try this recipe but can't track down zucchini flowers, wrap the cheese and anchovy in blanched spinach or roll in sautéed thin slices of eggplant before frying.

Melting Camembert Fritters on Gooseberry & Green Peppercorn Chutney

SERVES 4–6

12 ounces Camembert cheese, not too ripe

4 tablespoons unsalted butter

⅓ cup all-purpose flour, plus extra for coating

1½ cups milk, boiled & strained

3 egg yolks

1 teaspoon Dijon mustard

Freshly grated nutmeg

Salt & freshly ground black pepper

1 egg, beaten

2 cups fresh white bread crumbs

Vegetable oil for deep-frying

⅓ cup Gooseberry & Green Peppercorn Chutney (see page 186)

ALTERNATIVE CHEESES

Irish Cooleeney, Scottish Bonchester, Welsh Pencarreg or Sharpham

Don't expect these fritters to be anything like those breaded wedges of Camembert, deep-fried and served with a cloyingly sweet jam, that enjoyed inexplicable popularity on restaurant menus in the 1970s and 80s. Here, the fritters are made with a thick, well-flavored cheese sauce that has little cubes of Camembert stirred in to give a wonderful melting contrast. The accompanying chutney is refreshingly tart.

Remove the rind from the Camembert and cut the cheese into small pieces. Melt the butter in a pan over a low heat, stir in the flour, and cook for 2–3 minutes. Gradually add the boiled milk, stirring all the time, then bring to a boil and simmer gently for 5–10 minutes to give a thick sauce. Remove from the heat, add half the Camembert, and let the cheese melt in the sauce. Cool slightly, then beat in the egg yolks one at a time. Stir in the mustard and season with nutmeg, salt, and pepper. Stir in the remaining cheese. Pour into a greased shallow dish or a small baking pan. The mixture should be about ¾ inch deep. Let cool, then cover and chill for at least 4 hours, preferably overnight.

Remove the cheese mixture from the refrigerator and, using a 2-inch round cutter, cut out 12 disks. Coat them lightly in flour, dip in the beaten egg, and then coat in the bread crumbs.

Heat oil in a deep fryer or a large saucepan to 350°F. Fry the fritters a few at a time for 3–4 minutes, until golden. Drain on paper towels and serve immediately, accompanied by the chutney.

Carpaccio of Beef with Dolcelatte Mustard Dressing

SERVES 4

1-pound beef tenderloin

¼ cup olive oil

2 tablespoons coarse sea salt

Salt & freshly ground black pepper

12 ounces celery root

Juice of ½ lemon

3 tablespoons walnut oil

8 ounces corn salad (or mixed salad leaves)

For the dressing

1 egg yolk

2 tablespoons Dijon mustard

1 tablespoon white wine vinegar

1 teaspoon brown sugar

5 tablespoons vegetable oil

1 tablespoon finely chopped fresh dill, plus a few sprigs to garnish

2 ounces dolcelatte cheese

ALTERNATIVE CHEESES

Dunsyre Blue, Danish Blue, Blue Castello (Australia) or Unity Blue (Australia)

This mustard and blue cheese dressing makes a good alternative to the olive oil and Parmesan cheese that normally accompany carpaccio of beef. To make a warm carpaccio, use thin steaks—about ¼-inch thick—and grill over charcoal for about 1 minute per side.

Cut the beef tenderloin into wafer-thin slices across the grain. If you find it difficult to slice the meat this thinly, cut thicker slices, place them between 2 sheets of oiled plastic wrap and beat out carefully with a rolling pin or meat pounder. Spread the slices in a single layer over 4 large serving plates. Sprinkle with the olive oil, coarse salt, and some freshly ground black pepper.

For the dressing, put the egg yolk in a bowl and whisk in the mustard, vinegar, and sugar. Gradually add the oil in a thin stream, whisking all the time, as if making mayonnaise. Stir in the chopped dill. Put the dolcelatte in a separate bowl, pour on 2 tablespoons of boiling water, and mix to a smooth paste. Add this paste to the dressing, blending it in well. Adjust the seasoning carefully, as the dolcelatte will be quite salty.

Peel the celery root, then shred it coarsely or cut it into fine strips (a mandolin is useful for this). Put it in a bowl, toss with the lemon juice and walnut oil, and season to taste.

To serve, toss the corn salad with the dressing and arrange on top of the beef, then sprinkle the celery root over. Garnish with sprigs of dill.

P.G.TIPS

Chill the beef briefly in the freezer to make it easier to slice. If the prospect of slicing and salting the beef seems daunting, try using a cured meat such as Bresaola or even prosciutto—they both work well. The crisp, nutty texture of the celery root lends a special flavor to the dish. Make every effort to get hold of some; you will not be disappointed!

Chapter Two

SOUPS

Pear, Celery Root & Stilton Vichysoisse

SERVES 4

2 tablespoons unsalted butter

1 onion, finely diced

3 cups peeled & finely diced celery root

2 ripe pears, peeled, cored & finely diced

1 quart Chicken Stock (see page 16) or
Vegetable Stock (see page 16)

3 cups light cream

¾ cup crumbled Stilton cheese

2 tablespoons chopped fresh chives

Salt & freshly ground black pepper

ALTERNATIVE
CHEESES

Oregon Blue, Shropshire Blue, dolcelatte,
Milawa Blue (Australia) or Gippsland
Tarago River Blue (Australia)

Some people are quite purist about what should go in a vichysoisse, which traditionally is made with leek and potato, but I think this version is definitely worthy of consideration. Intense yet delicate in flavor, it makes an ideal soup for early autumn. Like the original, it's thickened with cream and served chilled, garnished with chives.

Heat the butter in a pan, add the onion and celery root, and cook over a gentle heat until they begin to soften, about 8–10 minutes. Stir in the pears and cook for 3–4 minutes. Add the stock and bring to a boil, then reduce the heat and simmer for 25 minutes, until the vegetables are tender. Remove from the heat and stir in the cream and Stilton. Purée the soup in a blender until smooth. Let cool, then chill thoroughly.

Before serving it may be necessary to thin down the soup with a little milk, stock, or cream. Stir in the chives and season to taste.

P.G. TIPS

I'm often asked what is the correct consistency for puréed soups. In my experience, a good general rule is that they should be approximately the consistency of light cream, that is thick enough to coat the back of a spoon.

Pea & Watercress Soup with Emmenthal Floating Islands

SERVES 4

4 tablespoons unsalted butter

½ cup roughly chopped onion

1 leek, roughly chopped

1 quart Chicken Stock
(see page 16)

3 cups shelled fresh or frozen peas

2 bunches of watercress, tough stems
removed

2 egg whites

¾ cup grated Emmenthal cheese,
plus extra to serve

2½ cups milk

⅔ cup heavy cream

Salt & freshly ground black pepper

These cloud-like cheese meringues not only taste great but also make a lovely presentation for this delicate, peppery-tasting pea soup.

Heat the butter in a heavy-based pan, add the onion and leek, and cook gently for 4–5 minutes, until softened. Add the stock and bring to a boil. Add the peas and simmer until tender—the cooking time will depend on whether you are using fresh or frozen peas. Stir in the watercress, then pour the soup into a blender and blitz until very smooth. For a more refined finish, strain it through a fine sieve afterwards.

Whisk the egg whites until they form stiff peaks and gently fold in the grated cheese. Use 2 tablespoons to shape the mixture into *quenelles*: To do this, take a heaped tablespoon of the mixture and then shape it with the second spoon, turning it between the two. Or, you can just scoop it into 8–12 balls. Bring the milk to a simmer in a large pan. Poach the *quenelles* in it for 3–4 minutes, until set, turning them over halfway through. Remove with a slotted spoon and drain well.

Add the cream to the soup and reheat without letting it boil, then season to taste. Pour into warm bowls and serve topped with the cheese meringues and some shavings of Emmenthal.

 P.G.TIPS
You could poach the floating islands in water, but they have a better flavor if you use milk. Save the milk to make a cheese sauce, if you like.

Potato & Wisconsin Cheddar Soup

SERVES 4

4 tablespoons unsalted butter

1½ pounds potatoes, cut into slices ½ inch thick

2½ cups thinly sliced leeks, white part only

3 garlic cloves, minced

2½ cups Chicken Stock (see page 16) or Vegetable Stock (see page 16)

⅓ cup heavy cream

1¼ cups milk, boiled & strained

1½ cups grated aged Wisconsin Cheddar cheese

Salt & freshly ground black pepper

ALTERNATIVE
CHEESES

Cantal Beaufort, Gruyère, or Emmenthal

Winter vegetables such as cabbage and carrots are often added to this soup along with the potatoes. I like to serve it with thin slices of toasted baguette rubbed with oil and garlic.

Heat the butter in a large saucepan and add the potatoes, leeks, and garlic. Cover and sweat for 4–5 minutes. Pour in the stock and bring to a boil. Skim to remove any impurities from the surface, then reduce the heat and simmer until the vegetables are just cooked. Add the cream and boiled milk and heat through gently, then stir in the grated cheese. Remove from the heat, season to taste, and serve.

Zuppa Pavese

SERVES 4

6 eggs

Salt & freshly ground black pepper

8 slices of white country-style bread, cut ½ inch thick

1 cup freshly grated Parmesan cheese

4 tablespoons unsalted butter

1 quart Meat Stock (see page 17) or, better still, consommé

This rustic Italian soup is very nourishing, and quick and easy to make. All you do is pour a well-flavored broth over slices of fried bread and then slip in an egg, which cooks in the heat of the broth. However, such simplicity relies on the finest ingredients for its success: Don't make the soup unless you have homemade stock, good country-style bread, and very fresh free-range eggs.

Beat 2 of the eggs in a bowl, season lightly, and pour into a shallow dish. Dip the bread slices in the beaten egg on both sides, then dredge them in ¾ cup of the grated Parmesan. Heat the butter in a large frying pan and fry the bread until golden on both sides.

Put the slices of fried bread in 4 deep, heatproof serving bowls. Bring the stock or consommé to a boil and pour it over the bread to immerse it completely. Crack an egg into each bowl on top of the bread. Leave the bowls on the side of the stove or over a very low heat to let the eggs cook lightly. Serve with the remaining cheese on the side, for sprinkling over the soup.

P.G. TIPS If you prefer, you can poach the eggs in the hot stock in a saucepan, then place them on the fried bread in the soup bowls and pour the soup over.

White Cabbage & Oyster Broth with Fourme d'Ambert Cheese

SERVES 4

4 tablespoons unsalted butter

2 heaped cups white cabbage cut into ¾-inch dice

1 teaspoon cumin seeds

1 quart Vegetable Stock (see page 16) or Chicken Stock (see page 16)

12 fresh oysters

2 ounces Fourme d'Ambert cheese

5 tablespoons heavy cream

Salt & freshly ground black pepper

1 tablespoon chopped fresh chives (optional)

ALTERNATIVE CHEESES

Dunsyre Blue or Cashel Blue

This soup dates back to my early days at Inigo Jones restaurant in London's Covent Garden. I enjoy preparing and tasting it as much now as I did then. You can make the soup without the oysters and it's still good, but they do give it an incomparable briny scent and flavor.

Melt the butter in a saucepan, add the cabbage, cover, and sweat for 5–8 minutes. Stir in the cumin seeds, pour in the stock, and bring to a boil. Skim off any impurities that rise to the surface, then simmer gently for about 15 minutes, until the cabbage is tender.

Meanwhile, open the oyster shells and remove the oysters, reserving their juice (see Tip on page 30). Cut the oysters in half, and strain the juice through a piece of cheesecloth. Set aside.

Press the Fourme d'Ambert cheese through a fine sieve and blend it with the cream. Stir the cream into the soup and adjust the seasoning. Add the cleaned oysters together with their strained juice, sprinkle with the chives, if using, and serve immediately.

P.G.TIPS

On no account let the soup boil after the cheese and cream mixture has been added to it or the delicate flavor will be spoiled. If the briny taste of oysters is not to your liking, you may prefer to substitute mussels. Simply cook the mussels with a little water until they open, then strain the cooking juices into the soup.

Cannellini Bean Soup with Fontina Gremolata

SERVES 4

4 tablespoons unsalted butter

½ cup diced onions

1 garlic clove, minced

1 cup dried cannellini beans, soaked overnight & drained

½ cup diced carrot

½ hot red chili pepper, seeded & minced

2 ripe tomatoes, chopped

2 cardamom pods, crushed

1 teaspoon cumin seeds

5½ cups Chicken Stock (see page 16) or Vegetable Stock (see page 16)

Salt & freshly ground black pepper

For the gremolata

¾ cup very finely grated fontina cheese

1 tablespoon finely grated lemon zest

1 tablespoon fresh thyme leaves

2 garlic cloves, minced

ALTERNATIVE
CHEESES

Raclette, Taleggio, or Port Salut

A warming, lightly spiced soup topped with stringy fontina cheese and spiked with lemon. Serve with chunks of fresh bread.

Melt the butter in a pan over a medium heat, add the onions and garlic, and sauté for 4–5 minutes, until softened. Add the cannellini beans, carrot, chili, and tomatoes, then cover and cook gently for 5 minutes. Next, stir in the cardamom, cumin seeds, and stock and bring to a boil. Reduce the heat and simmer for 1–1½ hours, or until the beans are tender. Pour the soup into a blender and blitz to a purée, then strain it through a fine sieve to give a creamy texture. Adjust the seasoning and reheat gently.

For the gremolata, mix all the ingredients together in a bowl. Pour the soup into warm bowls, scatter the gremolata over, and serve.

P.G. TIPS

Other legumes such as lentils can be used with just as good effect. I sometimes leave the beans whole and top them with the gremolata to serve as a winter stew.

Tomato Gazpacho with Cabécou-Stuffed Tomatoes

SERVES 4

2 pounds overripe plum tomatoes (or use half plum tomatoes, half beef tomatoes)

1 tablespoon tomato ketchup

1 tablespoon olive oil

1 small garlic clove, peeled

1 tablespoon sugar

⅔ cup Vegetable Stock
(see page 16)

A bunch of fresh basil

2 tablespoons red wine vinegar

2 tablespoons dry vermouth

Salt & freshly ground white pepper

For the stuffed tomatoes

2 Cabécou cheeses or other small, firm goat cheeses

½ onion, minced

1 small zucchini, minced

1 egg yolk

½ cup mixed fresh herbs, such as basil, chervil, parsley & chives, minced

2–3 tablespoons fresh white bread crumbs

8 ripe but firm small tomatoes

A little olive oil for brushing

The surprising thing about this recipe is the stunning contrast of hot and cold. The chilled smooth gazpacho is poured around stuffed tomatoes that have come straight from the oven. The soup is strongly scented with basil, which I love to use in large quantities, but you can always reduce the amount if you prefer or if you don't have much available.

For the soup, blanch the tomatoes in boiling water for 1 minute, then drain and refresh in ice water. Drain again and peel. Cut the tomatoes in half and put them in a bowl with the tomato ketchup, olive oil, garlic, sugar, vegetable stock, and leaves from the bunch of basil, reserving 8–12 leaves for garnishing the finished dish. Stir in the red wine vinegar and vermouth, season lightly, and let marinate for 1–2 hours.

Strain the tomato mixture through a fine sieve into a bowl, pressing hard to extract all the juice (don't use a blender or the fresh color of the tomatoes will be lost). Adjust the seasoning, then chill until ready to serve.

For the stuffed tomatoes, preheat the oven to 350°F. Put the goat's cheese in a bowl and crush with a fork. Stir in the onion, zucchini, egg yolk, and herbs, then add enough bread crumbs to bind the mixture lightly together. Season to taste. Slice a lid off the top of each tomato and reserve. Carefully scoop out the pulp and seeds from the tomatoes with a spoon. Fill them with the stuffing. Brush with a little olive oil and bake for 5 minutes, until soft and heated through.

Place 2 stuffed tomatoes in each soup plate and replace their lids, then carefully pour the gazpacho around. Decorate with the reserved basil leaves and serve immediately.

P.G. TIPS

Make this soup in late summer when overripe tomatoes are being sold off cheaply. I strongly recommend that you keep this delicate, fresh-tasting soup for the summer months, as tomatoes have less flavor, juice, and sweetness in winter.

Cauliflower Cheese Soup

SERVES 4

1 large head cauliflower, weighing about 1 pound 10 ounces

4 tablespoons unsalted butter

1 onion, thinly sliced

1 leek, thinly sliced

1 quart Vegetable Stock (see page 16) or water

2 egg yolks

¼ cup heavy cream

¾ cup grated Wisconsin Cheddar cheese

Freshly grated nutmeg

Salt & freshly ground black pepper

ALTERNATIVE

CHEESES

A soft goat cheese or Stilton

According to a recent survey, by far the most popular vegetable dish in the UK is cauliflower cheese. Let's face it, it's something we all enjoy. So why not try cauliflower cheese soup?

Trim the outer green leaves off the cauliflower and cut it into florets. Heat the butter in a heavy-based saucepan, add the onion and leek, cover, and cook gently for 2–3 minutes, until the vegetables begin to soften. Do not let them brown. Add the cauliflower florets (reserving a few small ones as a garnish) and cook gently for 4–5 minutes. Pour in the stock or water and bring to a boil, then reduce the heat and simmer for 20–25 minutes, until the cauliflower is very tender. Meanwhile, cook the reserved cauliflower florets in boiling salted water until just tender. Drain and refresh in cold water, then drain again well and reserve.

Purée the soup in a blender until smooth. Return it to the saucepan and bring to a boil. In a bowl, lightly whisk together the egg yolks, cream, and cheese. Whisk about 6 tablespoons of the soup into this mixture, then stir it back into the remainder of the soup; do not let it boil. Season with nutmeg, salt, and pepper, then serve garnished with the cooked cauliflower florets.

Kohlrabi &
Gorgonzola Soup

SERVES 4

2 tablespoons unsalted butter
2 kohlrabi, peeled & cut into small cubes
1 potato, peeled & cut into small cubes
1 quart Chicken Stock
(see page 16)
½ cup milk
½ cup heavycream
½ cup crumbled Gorgonzola cheese
Salt & freshly ground black pepper

ALTERNATIVE
CHEESES

Fourme d'Ambert, Gippsland Blue
(Australia), or Milawa Blue (Australia)

Kohlrabi is a strange and, in my view, much underrated vegetable. It looks like a turnip, but is in fact a member of the cabbage family. Its mild flavor is very good with Gorgonzola; however, if you can't find kohlrabi, you could substitute sweet potatoes, turnips, or cauliflower.

Heat the butter in a pan, add the kohlrabi and potato, and cook over a gentle heat for 2–3 minutes. Add the stock and bring to a boil, then reduce the heat and simmer for 20–25 minutes, until the vegetables are very soft. Purée the soup in a blender until smooth. Pour it back into the pan, add the milk and cream, and bring to a boil. Remove from the heat and stir in the Gorgonzola. Season to taste and serve.

Lobster & Vermont Cheddar Bisque

SERVES 4

1 cooked lobster, weighing about
1 pound 10 ounces

6 tablespoons unsalted butter

½ onion, roughly chopped

1 celery stalk, roughly chopped

1 carrot, roughly chopped

2 garlic cloves, minced

2 tablespoons tomato paste

¼ cup cognac

⅔ cup dry white wine

1 tablespoon fresh tarragon leaves, plus a
few sprigs to garnish

½ cup all-purpose flour

1 quart Chicken Stock
(see page 16)

⅔ cup heavy cream

¾ cup grated Vermont Cheddar cheese

Cayenne pepper

Salt & freshly ground black pepper

The bisque is also very good made with crab or langoustines (Dublin Bay prawns) instead of lobster.

Split the lobster in half down the back: The easiest way to do this is to put a large knife through the center of the body section and cut down through the head, then take out the knife, turn the lobster around, and cut down the center of the body through the tail. Remove and discard the head sac and the intestinal vein, then remove the cooked lobster meat from the head and tail. Crack the claws in 2 or 3 places and pick out the meat. Place the lobster shells in a bowl and, using a meat pounder, crush them into smallish pieces. This helps to extract maximum flavor.

Heat the butter in a heavy-based pan, add the crushed lobster shells, and fry for 4–5 minutes, until they begin to turn golden. Add the vegetables and garlic and fry for 5 minutes, until softened. Stir in the tomato paste, then add the cognac, white wine, and tarragon leaves. Cook for 5 minutes. Stir in the flour and cook for a further 5 minutes. Add the stock, bring to a boil, and skim off any impurities that rise to the surface. Reduce the heat and simmer for 30–40 minutes.

Meanwhile, dice the lobster meat and set aside. Bring the cream to a boil in a separate pan, then remove from the heat. Add the cheese and stir until melted and smooth, then set aside.

Blitz the soup in a blender until the shells are quite finely ground, then pass it through a very fine sieve. Stir in the cheese cream. Add cayenne, salt, and pepper to taste, then pour the soup into warm bowls. Garnish with the diced lobster meat and sprigs of tarragon, dust very lightly with cayenne, and serve.

P.G.TIPS Rice can be used instead of flour to thicken the soup. It is important that you do not cook the stock for longer than 40 minutes, as it will lose its natural flavors and become bitter. If you decide to use crab instead of lobster, cook the live crabs for 12–15 minutes, depending on their size.

Bread & Pecorino Soup

SERVES 4

1 quart Chicken Stock
(see page 16)

4 tablespoons olive oil

2 garlic cloves, minced

2 cups potatoes peeled, & cut into small
cubes

4 thick slices of stale Italian country
bread, cut into cubes

6 tablespoons grated pecorino cheese

1 tablespoon coarsely chopped fresh
marjoram

¼ teaspoon grated lemon zest

Salt

Cracked black pepper (see Tip on
page 146)

Like Zuppa Pavese (see page 54), this is an Italian peasant-style soup. I love the simplicity of it, made with just a few basic ingredients and a little care. It makes thrifty use of leftovers but it is essential to have good-quality stock. Good-quality olive oil is also a must, and you should not neglect the lemon; however strange it may sound, it really does give a little lift to this substantial, warming soup.

Bring the stock to a boil with 3 tablespoons of the olive oil. Add the garlic and potatoes and return to a boil. Add the bread cubes and simmer for 20–25 minutes, until the potatoes are tender.

Remove the pan from the heat and stir in the pecorino, marjoram, and lemon zest. Season with a little salt and a sprinkling of freshly cracked black pepper. Drizzle the remaining olive oil over and serve.

French Onion Soup with Beer & Camembert

SERVES 4

6 tablespoons unsalted butter

3 cups finely sliced onions

½ tablespoon sugar

1 tablespoon all-purpose flour

1 teaspoon tomato paste

½ cup light beer

1 quart Meat Stock (see page 17)

Salt & freshly ground black pepper

1 ficelle (small, thin baguette) or 2 crusty
bread rolls, thinly sliced & toasted

4 ounces Camembert cheese, rind
removed, thinly sliced

ALTERNATIVE

CHEESES

Carré de l'Est,
Gruyère, Emmenthal

This variation on the classic French onion soup replaces the usual white wine and Gruyère with ingredients from Normandy – beer and Camembert cheese. I have also successfully replaced the Camembert with Carré de l'Est, which is milder in flavor and has a delicate aroma when ripe. You can, of course, use grated Gruyère or Emmenthal for a more traditional onion soup.

Heat the butter in a heavy-based pan, add the onions and sugar, and cook over a medium heat for at least 20 minutes, until very soft, golden, and caramelized. Stir in the flour and tomato paste and cook for 2 minutes, until the onions brown very slightly. Pour in the beer, and bring to a boil. After 1 minute add the stock. Reduce the heat and simmer for 15–20 minutes. Season to taste.

Pour the soup into 4 heatproof soup bowls or 1 large tureen and float the toasted bread on top in a single layer. Cover this with the Camembert slices. Put the bowls under the broiler (or in a hot oven) until the cheese forms a well-browned crust. Serve immediately.

Saffron Vegetable Chowder with Cilantro & Goat Cheese Pesto

SERVES 4

3 tablespoons olive oil

1 garlic clove, minced

1 leek, 1 carrot, 1 celery stalk, 1 zucchini, and 1 potato, all cut into ¼-inch dice

1 quart Vegetable Stock (see page 16) or Chicken Stock (see page 16)

A pinch of saffron strands

2 tomatoes, skinned, seeded & cut into ¼-inch dice

2 tablespoons Cilantro & Goat Cheese Pesto (see page 20)

½ cup milk

Salt & freshly ground black pepper

A beautifully delicate vegetable chowder spiked with aromatic saffron and cilantro. Saffron is now much more readily available, and imports from Spain and the Middle East continue to improve. It is an expensive spice, but it has no substitute, especially in this chowder. Sachets of powdered saffron are cheaper than saffron strands, although they cannot compete with them in flavor—always buy the real thing.

Heat the olive oil in a heavy-based pan, together with the garlic. Next, add the leek, carrot, celery, zucchini, and potato and cook for 2 minutes over a low heat.

Add the stock and saffron and bring to a boil. Reduce the heat and simmer for 20–25 minutes, until the vegetables are tender. Add the tomatoes and pesto and stir thoroughly, then add the milk. Season to taste with salt and pepper and serve immediately.

P.G. TIPS

As an effective variation, replace the cilantro and goat cheese pesto with fresh herbs, such as parsley, basil, or chives.

Chapter Three

SALADS

Plum Tomato Salad with Goat's Milk Dressing

SERVES 4

8 large, ripe, but firm plum tomatoes, cut
into slices ¼ inch thick

Salt & freshly ground black pepper

3 ounces soft goat cheese

⅓ cup goat's milk

2 tablespoons strained plain yogurt

1 tablespoon chopped fresh basil

1 tablespoon chopped fresh oregano

½ tablespoon chopped fresh cilantro

The simplest of tomato salads, topped with a creamy dressing made with goat cheese and goat's milk. Serve as an accompaniment or as part of a selection of salads for a picnic.

Arrange the tomato slices in overlapping circles in a shallow serving bowl. Season with salt and pepper. Whisk all the remaining ingredients together and pour over the tomatoes. Serve well chilled.

P.G.TIPS If you can't find goat's milk, cow's milk works well, too. I personally see no gain in removing the tomato skins for this salad, especially in summer when tomatoes are at their best. It is, of course, a matter of choice, and others may like to blanch them briefly in boiling water before peeling off the skins. Chives, parsley, or chervil would make excellent alternative herbs, but they must be fresh.

Blackened Leek, Red Onion & Smoked Mozzarella Salad with Tarragon Vinaigrette

SERVES 4

A pinch of sugar

24 young leeks, trimmed

Salt & freshly ground black pepper

2 red onions, cut into wedges

1 smoked mozzarella cheese, cut into 8 thin slices

For the vinaigrette

3 tablespoons tarragon vinegar or champagne vinegar

1 teaspoon Dijon mustard

1 tablespoon chopped fresh tarragon

9 tablespoons extra-virgin olive oil

1 tomato, seeded & finely diced

1 tablespoon capers, rinsed & drained

1 tablespoon green olives, pitted & finely chopped

1 hard-boiled egg, chopped

ALTERNATIVE CHEESES

Buffalo mozzarella or a goat cheese, such as coarsely grated crottin

I love the smoky flavors that predominate in this salad. The tart vinaigrette makes an ideal dressing for the charred leeks. If possible, grill the vegetables over charcoal.

Bring a large pan of water to a boil with the sugar and a little salt. Throw in the leeks, return to a boil, and cook gently for 2–3 minutes. Drain them well and dry on a cloth.

For the vinaigrette, mix the vinegar, mustard, and tarragon together in a bowl, then whisk in the olive oil. Add all the remaining ingredients and season to taste with salt and pepper.

Grill the leeks and onions—or the best flavor this should be done over charcoal, but you can also cook them on a ridged cast-iron grill pan or under the broiler. When they are tender and slightly blackened, remove from the heat and season with salt and pepper.

Toss the leeks and onions with the vinaigrette and adjust the seasoning. Arrange on 4 serving plates. Drape 2 slices of mozzarella over each portion and serve.

P.G.TIPS

Smoked mozzarella may not be a recognized household cheese, yet for me it is one of the nicest smoked cheeses. It is worth seeking out. If you have a problem finding it, a creamy-tasting natural mozzarella would be fine.

Warm Lentil Salad with Pepper-Grilled Goat Cheese & Anchovy Toasts

SERVES 4

1 cup Puy lentils

1 onion, minced

1 teaspoon cumin seeds

¼ cup olive oil

2 tablespoons balsamic vinegar or white wine vinegar

1 shallot, minced

For the toasts

6 canned anchovy fillets, rinsed & dried

1 egg yolk

5 tablespoons olive oil

4 slices of French bread, cut ⅔ inch thick

4 Montrachet goat cheeses, cut in ½ inch slices

1 tablespoon fresh thyme or rosemary leaves

1 tablespoon coarsely ground black pepper

ALTERNATIVE
CHEESE

4 crottins, cut horizontally in half

The dark greeny-blue French lentilles du Puy are generally considered to have the best flavor and are well worth buying. They have recently been granted appellation d'origine contrôlée status, just like a fine wine or cheese, which means that only lentils from a particular corner of France—he area around Puy-en-Velay in the Haute Loire—are entitled to be called Puy. This decree is causing consternation among some British supermarket chains, which sell "Puy lentils" that have in fact been produced in Canada. If you can't get the genuine article, don't worry! Cannellini beans also work very well in this winter salad.

Put the lentils in a saucepan, cover with cold water, and bring to a boil, skimming off any impurities that rise to the surface. Add the onion and cumin seeds and simmer for 30–40 minutes, until the lentils are just tender. Drain them well. Mix the olive oil, vinegar, and shallot together and stir into the lentils. Keep warm.

For the cheese and anchovy toasts, work the anchovies and egg yolk to a paste with a mortar and pestle, then gradually blend in the olive oil to make a thick purée. Toast the French bread and spread with the anchovy paste, then top each one with 2 slices of goat cheese. Sprinkle with the thyme or rosemary leaves and black pepper and place under the broiler until lightly browned. Put the warm lentils on serving plates, top with the toasts, and serve.

P.G.TIPS Because the quantities for the anchovy paste are small, you really need to use a mortar and pestle. However, if you double the amount, you can blitz everything together in a blender. You are bound to find a use for the surplus; store it in the refrigerator and toss with pasta or use in sandwiches.

Spinach, Blue Cheese & Avocado Salad with Pumpkin Seeds

SERVES 4

12 ounces (about 3½ cups) tender young spinach leaves

1½ cups sliced mushrooms

2 hard-boiled eggs, chopped

¾ cup blue cheese, cut in ½-inch cubes

1 garlic clove, minced

scant 1 cup fromage blanc

1 teaspoon mild Dijon mustard

1 teaspoon lemon juice

Salt & freshly ground black pepper

1 avocado, peeled, pitted & cut into ½-inch cubes

12 slices of small baguette, toasted

½ cup pumpkin seeds, toasted

For me, the combination of spinach and blue cheese is a spectacular one. Any type of blue cheese is suitable for this wonderfully fresh-tasting salad, scattered with nutritious pumpkin seeds. Just use your favorite.

Put the spinach in a salad bowl and add the mushrooms, hard-boiled eggs, and blue cheese. Mix together the garlic, fromage blanc, mustard, and lemon juice to make a dressing and toss carefully with the salad. Season to taste.

Arrange on serving plates. Top with the avocado and toasted baguette slices and sprinkle the toasted pumpkin seeds over. Serve immediately.

P.G. TIPS Other vegetables, such as leeks, artichokes, and even asparagus, can be prepared in the same way for this salad. Pumpkin seeds are quite easy to find in healthfood shops, but sunflower seeds make a tasty alternative if necessary.

Salad of Pickled Herrings, Jarlsberg, Potatoes & Dill

SERVES 4

1 pound pickled herrings

5 ounces Jarlsberg cheese

1 pound waxy potatoes

1 red onion, minced

2 tablespoons white wine vinegar

6 tablespoons olive oil

1 tablespoon crème fraîche

2 tablespoons chopped fresh dill

1 tablespoon sweet German mustard

Salt & freshly ground black pepper

ALTERNATIVE
CHEESES

Emmenthal, Cheddar, Havarti, or Tilsit

Jarlsberg cheese is said by many to be a copy of the famous Swiss Emmenthal. I personally think it has a more delicate flavor and not such a nutty aftertaste. It is one of Norway's proudest treasures and deserves to be better known and more frequently used.

Cut the pickled herrings into large chunks and the Jarlsberg into sticks. Cook the potatoes in boiling salted water until just tender, then drain. Leave until cool enough to handle, then peel and cut in half. Put them in a bowl and add the herrings and red onion.

Mix together the vinegar, oil, crème fraîche, dill, and mustard to make a dressing. Pour the dressing over the potatoes, herrings, and onions and toss lightly together, then season to taste. Transfer to a serving bowl, top with the Jarlsberg, and serve.

Roquefort & Red Cabbage Salad with Roasted Walnut Vinaigrette

SERVES 4

¼ head red cabbage, central core removed, thinly sliced

¼ cup red wine vinegar

¼ cup sugar

2½ cups water

4 ounces (4 slices) streaky bacon, cut into ¾-inch dice

2 slices of white bread, cut into ½-inch cubes

1 garlic clove, minced

2 heads Belgian endive

1 small head radicchio

1 heaped cup crumbled Roquefort cheese

Salt & freshly ground black pepper

For the vinaigrette

¼ cup red wine vinegar

1 teaspoon Dijon mustard

¼ cup walnut oil

¼ cup olive oil

2 tablespoons roasted walnuts (see Tip) broken into chunks

ALTERNATIVE
CHEESES

Any blue cheese

I am very fond of this salad. It always finds a place on my winter menus and is extremely pretty. The crunch of red cabbage and roasted walnuts makes an excellent combination with the sharp and tangy Roquefort. If Roquefort is not available, any blue cheese could be substituted, but I find the stronger ones such as Gorgonzola work best.

Put the cabbage in a bowl. Bring the vinegar to a boil, add the sugar, and, once dissolved, pour it over the cabbage and stir well. Boil the water and pour that over the cabbage too. Leave to soak for 5 minutes, then drain in a colander and let cool.

Heat a frying pan over a high heat, add the bacon, and cook until it is crisp and the fat has been released. Add the bread and fry until golden, then stir in the garlic and fry for 1 minute. Remove from the heat. Put the red cabbage in a salad bowl with the endive and radicchio leaves. Scatter the bacon, croûtons and Roquefort cheese over.

Whisk together all the ingredients for the vinaigrette and pour it over the salad. Toss well, adjust the seasoning, and serve.

P.G.TIPS To roast nuts, toss them in a little oil, season lightly, and place on a baking sheet. Roast in an oven preheated to 350°F for 5–8 minutes, or until toasted in flavor and color. Cool before use. I have on occasion replaced the red cabbage with finely shredded beets: a great alternative summer salad.

Crab & Asparagus Salad with Lemon, Mustard & Parmesan Vinaigrette

SERVES 4

12 asparagus spears, peeled &
well trimmed

2 heads Belgian endive

2 avocados, peeled, pitted & sliced

2 carrots, cut into matchsticks

11 ounces (about 2 cups) fresh white
crabmeat

Parmesan cheese shavings, to garnish

*For the lemon, mustard & Parmesan
vinaigrette*

1 tablespoon Dijon mustard

1 medium egg yolk

1 tablespoon lemon juice

Finely grated zest of ¼ lemon

1 tablespoon champagne vinegar or
white wine vinegar

5 tablespoons extra-virgin olive oil

1½ tablespoons freshly grated Parmesan
cheese

Salt & freshly ground black pepper

Many years ago I worked in the West Country and discovered just how good fresh crab can be. It has an incomparable flavor. The salad makes a good first course for an early-summer meal.

Cook the asparagus spears in boiling salted water for 3–4 minutes or until just tender. Drain and refresh in cold water, then dry them thoroughly and cut lengthwise in half.

For the dressing, whisk together the mustard, egg yolk, lemon juice and zest, and vinegar, then whisk in the olive oil. Add the grated Parmesan cheese and season to taste.

Pull the leaves from the endive, wash and dry them, and arrange in a salad bowl or on serving plates. Put the asparagus, avocado, carrots, and crabmeat in a separate bowl and toss gently with the dressing, then adjust the seasoning. Scatter this mixture over the endive leaves. Sprinkle with some coarsely cracked black pepper (see Tip on page 146) then scatter the Parmesan shavings over the top. Serve immediately.

P.G.TIPS Vegetarians can easily omit the crabmeat and replace it with more vegetables. Globe artichoke hearts, for example, would go rather well.

Chili-Pickled Orange, Feta & Olive Salad

SERVES 4

4 oranges, preferably navel

⅓ cup white wine vinegar

3 tablespoons sugar

1 hot red chili pepper, thinly sliced into rings

⅓ cup olive oil

Salt & freshly ground black pepper

2 tablespoons black olives, pitted

¾ cup feta cheese cut into ½-inch cubes

1 tablespoon chopped fresh oregano or parsley

Baby spinach and arugula leaves, to garnish (optional)

ALTERNATIVE

CHEESES

Haloumi or a firm goat cheese

In this tangy salad the oranges are marinated in vinegar and sugar overnight to give a refreshing sweet-and-sour flavor. Feta is a much-copied cheese and consequently the quality and flavor vary greatly, as does the type of milk used. Always try to obtain genuine Greek feta, which is generally made of 30 percent goat's milk and 70 percent sheep's milk.

Peel the oranges, being sure to remove all the white pith, and cut them into slices ¼ inch thick. Remove any seeds. Put the orange slices in a shallow dish. Boil the vinegar and sugar together for 2–3 minutes, then add the chili and pour over the orange slices. Cover and leave overnight.

The next day, drain off the juices from the pickled oranges into a bowl. Whisk in the olive oil to make a dressing and season with salt and pepper. Arrange the oranges in a serving bowl. Stir the olives, feta, and oregano or parsley into the dressing and sprinkle it over the oranges. Sprinkle with coarsely cracked black pepper (see Tip on page 146). Scatter the spinach and arugula leaves, if using, over the top and serve.

P.G.TIPS

Some people like to soak feta cheese in warm water or milk before using. This effectively softens the strong, salty flavor.

Radicchio, Mushroom & Chive Salad with Blue Cheese-Yogurt Dressing

SERVES 4

2 heads radicchio
5 cups sliced button mushrooms
1 bunch of fresh chives

For the blue cheese-yogurt dressing
2 ounces Stilton cheese
1 tablespoon champagne vinegar
5 tablespoons crème fraîche
3 tablespoons strained plain yogurt
Juice of ½ lemon
Freshly grated nutmeg
Salt & freshly ground black pepper
1 tablespoon chopped fresh chives

ALTERNATIVE
CHEESES

Roquefort, dolcelatte, or Cambazola

Radicchio is a bitter salad leaf that to my mind needs a contrasting partner. The blue cheese-yogurt dressing fits the bill perfectly. You could add some chopped hard-boiled egg, potatoes, and haricot verts to make a more substantial dish for a main course.

First make the dressing. Put the Stilton in a bowl and mash well with a fork. Stir in the vinegar, then gently whisk in the crème fraîche and yogurt. Squeeze in the lemon juice and season to taste with nutmeg, salt, and pepper. Fold in the chives.

Separate the radicchio leaves, wash them, and dry them well. Place in a bowl, add the sliced mushrooms, and season lightly. Add the blue cheese dressing and toss carefully, then adjust the seasoning to taste. Arrange on serving plates. Snip the chives into pieces ½ inch long and scatter over the top. Serve immediately.

P.G. TIPS

If you prefer a less tart dressing, add 1 tablespoon warmed honey, maple syrup, or even good old sugar. Try adding a little grated orange zest to the dressing, too. Belgian endive has a similar bitter taste and could easily be substituted for the radicchio.

Insalata di Fontina

SERVES 4

8 ounces new potatoes

2 ounces prosciutto, cut into strips

4 ounces fontina cheese, cut into sticks

2 ounces mortadella, cut into sticks

6 cocktail gherkins, cut lengthwise into quarters

1 red onion, sliced into thin rings

For the dressing

1 tablespoon chopped fresh oregano

¼ teaspoon Dijon mustard

2 canned anchovy fillets

2 tablespoons white wine vinegar

6 tablespoons olive oil

Salt & freshly ground black pepper

ALTERNATIVE
CHEESES

Gruyère, Emmenthal, Port Salut, or Tête de Moine

This hearty salad of cheese, ham, and potatoes is substantial enough to serve as a main course. Salads that combine cheese and meat are very common in northern Europe. I devised this one with Italian flavorings in mind. The recipe has been in my repertoire since my early days as a chef and has remained one of my favorite salads. The original salad consists of shavings of Tête de Moine (monk's head), a cheese native to Switzerland. It is rather expensive and a little difficult to find except in specialist cheese shops, but well worth enquiring about. Fontina makes a more accessible and good substitute.

For the dressing, place the oregano and mustard in a small bowl. Rinse the anchovy fillets to reduce their salty flavor, then drain. Dry them well and mince. Add them to the bowl along with the vinegar and mix well together. Add the olive oil and whisk to form a light dressing. Season to taste and set aside.

Cook the potatoes in boiling salted water for about 20 minutes until just tender, then drain and cool slightly before peeling. Cut into ¼ inch thick slices and place in a bowl. While the potatoes are still warm, pour the dressing over and leave for 20 minutes to let them soak up the flavors.

Add the remaining ingredients and mix together. Adjust the seasoning and serve.

Salad of Grilled Lamb Fillet with St. Agur & Warm Mint Dressing

SERVES 4

4 boneless neck of lamb fillets, about 3 ounces each

4 ounces haricot verts

8–12 thin slices cut from a ficelle loaf or small baguette

Olive oil, for brushing

A handful each of curly endive & spinach leaves

2 tomatoes, skinned, seeded & cut into strips

1 cup thinly sliced button mushrooms

½ cup diced St. Agur cheese

For the dressing

¼ cup heavy cream

1 tablespoon honey

½ cup crumbled St. Agur cheese

1 tablespoon sherry vinegar

2 tablespoons olive oil

1 tablespoon chopped fresh mint

2 tablespoons hot water

Salt & freshly ground black pepper

ALTERNATIVE
CHEESES

Stilton, Danish Blue, Bleu d'Auvergne, or King Island (Australia)

Lamb and mint form a combination that everyone knows. I took it a stage further to create this wonderful salad.

Season the lamb fillets and grill on a ridged cast-iron grill pan (or cook under the broiler or in a frying pan) for 5–8 minutes, until done but still rosy inside. Keep warm.

Meanwhile, cook the beans in boiling salted water until just tender, then drain and refresh in cold water. Drain again and dry.

For the dressing, put the cream and honey in a pan and bring to a boil, then remove from the heat. Add the cheese and allow it to melt into the cream. Whisk in the vinegar, olive oil, and mint, then whisk in the water and season to taste.

Brush the slices of bread with olive oil and toast on both sides on the grill pan or under the broiler until they are lightly browned.

Put the curly endive and spinach leaves in a bowl. Add the tomatoes, beans, mushrooms, and cheese, then toss with the warm dressing. Put in the center of 4 serving plates. Slice the grilled lamb fillets and arrange around the salad. Top the salad with the croûtons and serve immediately.

Chapter Four

Tagliatelle with Fried Egg, Capers & Pecorino Sardo

SERVES 4

1 pound tagliatelle

Freshly grated nutmeg

Salt & freshly ground black pepper

3 tablespoons unsalted butter

2 tablespoons capers, rinsed & drained

4 free-range eggs

A little clarified butter (see Tip)

4 ounces pecorino sardo cheese, cut into shavings

A great and simple dish. When all that is needed is something quick but tasty, this fits the bill perfectly. Try adding crisply fried, diced pancetta to the pasta.

Cook the pasta in boiling salted water until *al dente*, then drain well and return to the pan. Season with nutmeg, salt, and pepper, add the butter and capers, and toss together well. Keep warm.

Quickly fry the eggs in clarified butter and season with salt. Arrange the pasta on warmed serving plates, top each portion with a fried egg, and scatter the pecorino shavings over. Sprinkle with a little freshly cracked black pepper (see Tip on page 146) and serve.

P.G. TIPS To clarify butter, heat gently in a small pan until it begins to boil. Boil for 2 minutes, then pour off the clear butter through a fine conical strainer or a cheesecloth-lined sieve, leaving the white, milky sediment in the pan. Store clarified butter in the refrigerator.

Baked Bucatini with Garlic Cheese & Ricotta Sauce

SERVES 4

2 tablespoons extra-virgin olive oil

1 small garlic clove, minced

⅔ cup herb & garlic Boursin

½ cup ricotta cheese

⅔ cup crème fraîche

⅓ cup light cream

2 tablespoons chopped fresh basil

Salt & freshly ground black pepper

1 pound bucatini

Freshly grated nutmeg

¾ cup freshly grated Parmesan cheese

ALTERNATIVE

CHEESE

Herb and garlic roulé

I have very strong views on cheeses with added flavorings and don't normally approve of them. In fact, you will find only this and one other recipe (see page 168) using them in this book. But I am very fond of Boursin, partly because my parents liked it and it was always in our refrigerator at home.

Preheat the oven to 400°F. Heat half the olive oil in a pan, add the garlic, and sweat until softened. Stir in the Boursin, ricotta, crème fraîche, and light cream and cook for 1 minute. Stir in the chopped basil and season with salt and pepper.

Cook the bucatini in boiling salted water until *al dente*, then drain well. Return to the pan, stir in the remaining olive oil, and season with nutmeg, salt, and pepper. Transfer the pasta to a baking dish and pour the cheese sauce over. Sprinkle the grated Parmesan on top and bake for about 10 minutes, until golden.

Stuffed Macaroni al Forno with Swiss Chard & Italian Cheeses

1 pound large macaroni, about
¾ inch in diameter

¾ cup crumbled dolcelatte cheese

¼ cup freshly grated Parmesan cheese

For the stuffing

6 tablespoons unsalted butter

1 onion, minced

5 ounces prosciutto, chopped (1½ cups)

1 pound Swiss chard, roughly shredded
(about 7 cups)

½ heaped cup ricotta cheese

1 cup freshly grated Parmesan cheese

1 egg yolk

Freshly grated nutmeg

Salt & freshly ground black pepper

For the sauce

4 tablespoons unsalted butter

⅓ cup all-purpose flour

2¼ cups milk, boiled & strained

ALTERNATIVE
CHEESES

Any mild blue cheese is fine for this dish
instead of the dolcelatte

*S*wiss chard was a very common vegetable in Britain in Victorian times and then fell into obscurity, but happily it is now regaining its popularity. It resembles spinach in flavor and is in season from September to March. Look out for red chard, with its striking beet-colored leaves, as a change from the green variety.

Preheat the oven to 400°F. For the stuffing, heat the butter in a pan over a medium heat, add the onion, and cook until lightly golden. Add the prosciutto and cook for 1 minute, then stir in the shredded chard and sweat for 3–4 minutes, until there is no moisture left in the pan. Transfer to a bowl and let cool. Meanwhile, cook the macaroni in plenty of boiling salted water until *al dente*, then drain and dry well.

Add the ricotta, Parmesan, and egg yolk to the cooled Swiss chard mixture and stir together well. Season with nutmeg, salt, and pepper. Put the mixture in a pastry bag fitted with a plain nozzle and use to fill the macaroni. Put them in a well-buttered shallow baking dish and set aside.

To make the sauce, melt the butter in a pan, add the flour, and stir for 1–2 minutes to form a *roux*. Gradually stir in the milk until you have a smooth sauce, then let cook for 8–10 minutes over a very low heat. Season to taste with nutmeg, salt, and pepper.

Pour the sauce over the stuffed macaroni, then sprinkle the dolcelatte and Parmesan over the top. Bake for 10–12 minutes or until a light golden crust forms. Let rest for 5 minutes before serving.

Topfenravioli with Prosciutto, Spinach & Foaming Brown Butter

SERVES 4

6 tablespoons unsalted butter

1 pound young spinach leaves (about 4½ cups)

½ cup cottage cheese, well drained

3 ounces prosciutto, finely diced (about ¾ cup)

¼ cup finely diced buffalo or cow's milk mozzarella cheese

2 tablespoons freshly grated Parmesan cheese, plus extra to serve

10 fresh basil leaves, roughly chopped, plus a few whole leaves to garnish

Freshly grated nutmeg

Salt & freshly ground black pepper

For the pasta dough
2 cups all-purpose flour

A pinch of salt

1 tablespoon extra-virgin olive oil

2 eggs plus 1 egg yolk, lightly beaten

ALTERNATIVE

CHEESE

You can use pot or farmer's cheese instead of well-drained cottage cheese.

Crumbly cottage or curd cheese is used extensively in many German dishes. I particularly like the stuffing for this ravioli.

First make the pasta dough. Put the flour, salt, and olive oil into a food processor and process for a few seconds to combine. Add the beaten eggs and process until the mixture forms a mass. This should only take a few seconds; it is important not to overwork the dough. Remove the dough from the food processor. It should be fairly soft and pliable. If it is too dry, knead in a little water; if it is too wet, sprinkle with a little flour. Cover with plastic wrap and let rest at room temperature for 15–30 minutes.

Meanwhile, make the filling. Heat 2 tablespoons of the butter in a large pan, add the spinach, and cook for just a few minutes, until it has wilted and all the excess moisture has evaporated. Transfer to a bowl and let cool, then mince. Stir in the cottage cheese, prosciutto, mozzarella, Parmesan, and chopped basil. Season to taste with nutmeg, salt, and pepper.

Roll out the dough using a pasta machine if you have one. Alternatively, divide it into 2 batches and roll it out very thinly by hand. It should be so thin that it is almost translucent. Lightly brush 1 sheet of the dough with water, then put teaspoonfuls of stuffing on it about 2 inches apart, in rows. Cover with the second sheet of pasta and press down gently, then cut around the stuffing with a 2½-inch fluted round pastry cutter. Check that the edges of the ravioli are well sealed.

Cook the ravioli in plenty of gently simmering salted water for 2–3 minutes, until *al dente*, then drain well. Heat the remaining butter in a frying pan until it is foaming and golden brown and smells nutty (the bottom of the pan will be covered with brown butter specks). Immediately drizzle the butter over the ravioli and sprinkle with more freshly grated Parmesan and a few basil leaves before serving.

Rigatoni with Mixed Peppers & Cilantro & Goat Cheese Pesto

SERVES 4

4 sweet peppers (1 red, 1 green, 1 yellow, 1 orange)

4 tablespoons unsalted butter

2 tablespoons olive oil

A pinch of sugar

Salt & freshly ground black pepper

1 pound rigatoni

1 quantity of Cilantro & Goat Cheese Pesto (see page 20)

Fresh cilantro leaves, to garnish (optional)

For an all-green version of this colorful pasta dish, you could substitute zucchini, leeks, and broccoli for the peppers.

Halve and seed the peppers, then cut them into strips ¼ inch wide. Heat the butter and oil in a frying pan, add the pepper strips, and cook gently for 10–15 minutes. If they begin to stick to the pan, add a little water. When the peppers are tender, stir in the sugar, and salt and pepper to taste.

Cook the rigatoni in a large pan of boiling salted water until *al dente*, then drain well. Stir the pasta into the peppers, add the pesto sauce, and lightly toss together. Adjust the seasoning, garnish with cilantro leaves, if desired, and serve.

P.G.TIPS
For a really quick sauce, use bottled peppers (pimientos) in oil. For a little variation why not try adding a few sautéed bacon *lardons* to the cooked pasta? Any other shaped pasta would look pretty in this dish.

Pennette al Dolcelatte

SERVES 4

1 pound pennette

⅓ cup heavy cream

½ cup Chicken Stock (see page 16) or Vegetable Stock (see page 16)

⅔ cup crumbled dolcelatte cheese

¼ cup extra-virgin olive oil

Freshly grated nutmeg

Salt & freshly ground black pepper

Freshly grated Parmesan cheese, to serve (optional)

ALTERNATIVE

CHEESE

Try torta di Gordenza, which is a combination of mascarpone and Gorgonzola, and omit the cream

Although I have used pennette for this dish, any type of pasta can be substituted. To offset the richness of the sauce, I sometimes top the pasta with a light herb salad of basil, chives, and oregano, mixed with a little curly endive and dressed with balsamic vinaigrette.

Cook the pennette in plenty of boiling salted water until *al dente*. Meanwhile, bring the cream and stock to a boil, then remove from the heat and stir in the dolcelatte until smooth. Whisk in the olive oil to form a light sauce.

Drain the pasta and return it to the saucepan. Season with nutmeg, salt, and pepper, then toss the pasta with the sauce. Serve immediately, with grated Parmesan, if desired.

RIGATONI WITH
MIXED PEPPERS & CILANTRO
& GOAT CHEESE PESTO

Bel Paese Calzoni

SERVES 4

1 quantity of risen pizza dough
(see opposite)

Flour, for dusting

2 tablespoons ricotta cheese

2 garlic cloves, minced

2 tablespoons olive oil

3 ounces Bel Paese cheese, rind removed,
coarsely chopped (about ⅓ cup)

4 ounces mortadella or prosciutto,
coarsely chopped (about 1 cup)

Salt & freshly ground black pepper

A little beaten egg

Vegetable oil for deep-frying (optional)

Calzone, which literally means pair of trousers!, is a sort of folded pizza, rather like a turnover. It is particularly delicious if you include lots of cheese, so the molten cheese spills out when you cut into it. You can vary the fillings to your own taste—try mozzarella, salami, or vegetables.

Punch down the risen dough, then roll it out thinly on a floured surface. Cut out eight 6-inch disks.

Mix together the ricotta, garlic, olive oil, Bel Paese, and chopped mortadella or prosciutto. Season to taste. Put the mixture on one half of each disk of dough, leaving a border. Brush the edges of the dough with beaten egg and fold over to make turnovers. Crimp the edges for a neat finish.

Heat vegetable oil in a large saucepan and fry the *calzoni* a few at a time for 5–6 minutes, until golden. Alternatively, brush them with a little beaten egg and bake in an oven preheated to 400°F for about 12–15 minutes. Serve hot.

The Ultimate Vegetarian Calzoni

SERVES 4

1 quantity of risen pizza dough
(see opposite)

Flour, for dusting

6 tablespoons olive oil

1 garlic clove, minced

¼ teaspoon fennel seeds

1 eggplant, peeled & thinly sliced

1 fennel bulb, thinly sliced

5 ounces mozzarella cheese, thinly sliced

10 basil leaves, roughly chopped

Salt & freshly ground black pepper

A little beaten egg

Vegetable oil for deep-frying (optional)

To me, these calzoni are lifted out of the ordinary by the inclusion of fennel, a much underrated vegetable which only the Italians seem to use to any great extent. Serve the calzoni with a tomato sauce, if you like.

Punch down the risen dough, then roll it out thinly on a floured surface. Cut out eight 6-inch disks.

For the filling, heat the olive oil in a pan with the garlic and fennel seeds. Add the eggplant and fennel slices and cook gently for 12–15 minutes, until golden and tender. Add a little water to the vegetables if they begin to stick to the pan. Transfer to a bowl and let cool, then add the mozzarella and basil. Season to taste. Fill the turnovers, seal with a little beaten egg, and cook as in the preceding recipe.

Roasted Vegetable Pizza with Goat Cheese, Mozzarella & Rosemary Oil

SERVES 4

1 red sweet pepper
⅓ cup olive oil
1 zucchini, thickly sliced
1 globe artichoke bottom, cooked & cut into quarters
8 small, flat mushrooms, stems removed
Salt & freshly ground black pepper
¼ cup tomato purée
12 cherry tomatoes, cut in half
½ cup goat cheese cut into ½-inch cubes
½ cup mozzarella cheese cut into ½-inch cubes

For the dough
2 teaspoons active dry yeast
1¼ cups water
4 cups all-purpose flour
1 teaspoon salt
2 tablespoons olive oil

For the rosemary oil
1 garlic clove, minced
2 tablespoons chopped fresh rosemary
⅓ cup extra-virgin olive oil

A truly wonderful vegetarian pizza: roasted vegetables topped with contrasting cheeses and drizzled with rosemary oil. A real treat.

For the dough, dissolve the yeast in a little of the water. Sift the flour and salt into a bowl and make a well in the center. Pour the yeast liquid into the well with the remaining water and the olive oil and bring it all together with your hands to form a pliable dough. Knead on a lightly floured surface for 6–8 minutes, until smooth and elastic. Place the dough in a lightly oiled bowl, cover with a damp cloth, and let rise at warm room temperature for 1 hour or until doubled in size.

Meanwhile, prepare the topping. Preheat the oven to 350°F. Brush the red pepper with a little of the olive oil, place in a baking dish, and roast for 20 minutes. Add the remaining oil to the dish and put the zucchini, artichoke, and mushrooms in it. Season with salt and pepper and return to the oven to roast for about 25 minutes or until all the vegetables are tender. Remove and let cool. Peel the pepper, cut it in half, and remove the seeds. Cut the flesh into strips and set aside.

For the rosemary oil, blitz together the garlic and rosemary with the oil in a blender and set aside.

Raise the oven temperature to 400°F. Punch down the dough, divide it into 4 pieces, and roll out each one into a 7-inch disk (or if you're in a party mood, make one big pizza). Spread one quarter of the tomato purée over each pizza base, then top with the roasted vegetables and the halved cherry tomatoes. Scatter both cheeses over the vegetables and drizzle the rosemary oil over. Bake for 15–20 minutes, until golden, then serve immediately.

Oyster & Spinach Pizza with Chorizo Sausage & Melting Dolcelatte

SERVES 4

6 tablespoons olive oil

2 red onions, thinly sliced

1 pound fresh spinach, washed

Salt & freshly ground black pepper

16 fresh oysters, shucked
(see Tip on page 30)

1 quantity of risen pizza dough
(see page 91)

8-9 ounces Spanish chorizo sausage,
thinly sliced

¾ cup crumbled dolcelatte cheese

ALTERNATIVE
CHEESES

Replace the dolcelatte with some shaved
pecorino or Gruyère.

Dolcelatte and chorizo, a spicy Spanish sausage, make a delicious combination. Add the saltiness and soft texture of oysters and you have a creative and full-flavored pizza.

Preheat the oven to 400°F. Heat 2 tablespoons of the oil in a pan, add the onions, and fry for 10–12 minutes, until lightly golden. Season and remove from the pan. Heat half the remaining oil in the pan, add the spinach, and cook for 2–3 minutes, until wilted. Season with salt and pepper and remove from the pan. Finally, add the rest of the oil to the pan and sauté the oysters for about 1 minute, just enough to seal them. Season and set aside.

Punch down the pizza dough and roll out into four 7-inch disks as in the preceding recipe. Distribute the spinach evenly over the pizza bases. Arrange slices of chorizo on top, then dice the oysters and scatter them over. Scatter the red onions on top and, lastly, the crumbled dolcelatte. Bake for 15 minutes or until the cheese is melted and bubbly. Serve immediately.

Suppli alla Gorgonzola con Basilico

SERVES 4

4 tablespoons olive oil

1 onion, minced

1 garlic clove, minced

1 heaped cup Arborio rice

2¼ cups Chicken Stock (see page 16) or Cheese-Infused Chicken Stock (see page 16)

4 tablespoons unsalted butter

¾ cup freshly grated Parmesan cheese

A good handful of fresh basil leaves

Freshly grated nutmeg

Salt & freshly ground black pepper

3 ounces Gorgonzola cheese

3 tablespoons all-purpose flour

2 eggs, beaten

2 cups fresh white bread crumbs

Vegetable oil for deep-frying

These little rice fritters are a specialty of Campania, where they are made with mozzarella and known as suppli al telefono, *meaning telephone wires, because the molten cheese forms long strings when the fritters are cut open. My version is made with basil and creamy Gorgonzola, so you don't get the stringy effect of the cheese, but you do get a wonderful, melting blue cheese fondue in the center. Serve on a pool of tomato sauce.*

Heat half the olive oil in a heavy-based pan, add the onion and garlic, and cook over a gentle heat until tender but not browned. Add the rice and stir well. Heat the stock to simmering point in a separate pan. Add a little of the stock to the rice and stir until it has been absorbed. Keep adding the stock, a ladleful at a time, stirring constantly, until the rice is tender but still firm to the bite. Stir in the butter and Parmesan, then spread the mixture out in a large baking pan and let cool.

Put the basil leaves in a blender (reserving a few to garnish the finished dish), add the remaining olive oil, and blitz to a thickish purée. Stir the purée into the cooled rice. Season to taste with nutmeg, salt, and pepper. Chill for at least 2 hours, preferably overnight.

To make the *suppli*, shape the rice mixture into 12–16 balls. Cut the Gorgonzola into 12–16 pieces and push a piece into the center of each rice ball. Re-form them neatly, pulling the rice back over the cheese and making sure it is completely enclosed. Coat the rice balls in the flour, then in the beaten egg and, finally, in the bread crumbs.

Heat vegetable oil in a deep fryer or a deep saucepan and fry the *suppli* in batches for 2–3 minutes, until golden. Drain well on paper towels and then serve immediately, garnished with the reserved basil.

P.G.TIPS

Suppli can also be made with plain boiled rice and can be stuffed with a variety of fillings, one of my favorites being a mixture of sautéed chicken livers, prosciutto, and wild mushrooms. For a vegetarian option, try sun-dried tomatoes and sautéed eggplant, and, of course, use vegetable stock instead.

Asparagus Risotto with Fonduta

SERVES 4

16 asparagus spears, peeled & well trimmed

9 tablespoons unsalted butter

2 shallots, minced

1 heaped cup Arborio rice

2½ cups Cheese-Infused Chicken Stock (see page 17)

⅓ cup dry white wine

Salt & freshly ground black pepper

For the fonduta

7 ounces fontina cheese, rind removed, thinly sliced

5 tablespoons milk

1 tablespoon unsalted butter

2 egg yolks

1½ tablespoons heavy cream

ALTERNATIVE
CHEESES

Beaufort, Jarlsberg, Gruyère, or Emmenthal

Fonduta is one of Italy's great classic sauces and I use it a lot with pasta and vegetables. Here it makes a creamy addition to an asparagus risotto. Lightly sautéed wild mushrooms can be stirred into the risotto with the asparagus for added flavor, if desired.

For the *fonduta*, put the cheese in a pan with the milk and leave for 2 hours.

Meanwhile, cook the asparagus in boiling salted water for 5 minutes or until just tender. Drain, refresh in cold water, and then dry. Cut into thin diagonal slices and set aside.

Put the butter for the *fonduta* in a stainless steel or glass bowl set over a pan of gently simmering water, making sure the water does not touch the base of the bowl. When it has melted, add the milk-soaked cheese. Stir until the cheese has melted and the mixture has become more solid. Stir in the egg yolks, one at a time. At this stage the mixture will become runny again. Stir constantly until the sauce has thickened, making sure it does not become too hot, otherwise it will curdle. Add the cream and keep warm.

For the risotto, melt 8 tablespoons of the butter in a saucepan, add the shallots, and cook gently until softened but not browned. Add the rice and stir until coated with the butter. Heat the stock to simmering point in a separate pan. Add the white wine and a little of the stock to the rice and stir until the liquid has been absorbed. Keep adding the stock, a ladleful at a time, stirring constantly, until the rice is tender but still retains a bite. Toward the end of cooking, add the stock in smaller quantities and check if the rice is done. It should take about 25 minutes in all.

Add enough of the *fonduta* to the risotto to give a loose but not sloppy consistency. Melt the remaining butter in a pan and quickly reheat the asparagus in it. Stir the asparagus into the risotto and adjust the seasoning. Divide among 4 serving plates. Serve immediately.

P.G.TIPS I like asparagus to be well trimmed before cooking. Snap off the woody part from the base of each spear, then peel away the skin from the base to the bud at the tip. The older and coarser the asparagus, the more trimming it will need.

Crispy Cheese Risotto al Salto

SERVES 4

2 cups leftover risotto
¼ cup freshly grated Parmesan cheese
½ cup grated fontina or Emmenthal cheese
Salt & freshly ground black pepper
3 tablespoons vegetable oil
1 tablespoon unsalted butter, melted

This is a very good way of using up leftover risotto, and, in fact, it is worth making extra just for this. A crispy fried risotto cake, it makes an ideal accompaniment to a classic osso buco in a rich tomato sauce, or you can serve it with grilled vegetables for a vegetarian dish.

Mix the cooked risotto with both cheeses and season well with salt and pepper. Heat a heavy-based frying pan over a high heat. Add the oil and then the rice and cheese mixture, packing it down well to form a cake about ½–¾ inch thick. Reduce the heat and cook for about 5 minutes, until golden and crisp around the edges. Turn the cake over and cook for a further 5 minutes, until golden and crisp. Turn out onto a serving dish, brush with the melted butter, and serve cut into wedges.

Baked Walnut Gnocchi with Asiago & Gruyère

SERVES 4

12 ounces boiling potatoes, peeled & cut into chunks (about 3 cups)
¾ cup ground walnuts
¾ cup grated Asiago cheese
1 tablespoon unsalted butter
2 egg yolks
scant 1 cup all-purpose flour
Freshly grated nutmeg
Salt & freshly ground black pepper

For the topping
4 tablespoons unsalted butter
1 tablespoon roughly chopped fresh flat-leaf parsley
½ cup finely grated Gruyère cheese
¼ cup finely grated Asiago cheese

Walnuts and nutty-flavored Gruyère are a great combination and this makes an excellent dish for autumn. For a real treat, sauté some fresh cèpes or porcini (Boletus edulis) with garlic and parsley, then put them on top of the poached gnocchi before adding the two cheeses.

Cook the potatoes in boiling salted water until tender, then drain well. Mash them while they are still hot. Add the walnuts and Asiago and beat well to help the cheese to melt. Mix in the butter, egg yolks, and half the flour, then season with nutmeg, salt, and pepper. Turn the mixture out onto a lightly floured work surface and knead in the remaining flour, a little at a time, to form a smooth, soft, but not sloppy dough. Let cool.

Roll out the dough into long cylinders 1 inch thick and cut them into ¾-inch lengths. Roll each piece over the prongs of a fork to form the classic ridged and slightly curved gnocchi shape. Place the gnocchi on a floured baking sheet and let them dry for about 1 hour.

Preheat the oven to 350°F. Poach the gnocchi, a few at a time, in a large pan of boiling salted water until they rise to the surface, about 2–3 minutes. Remove with a slotted spoon and arrange in a lightly greased, shallow baking dish.

For the topping, melt the butter and pour it over the gnocchi, then sprinkle them with the parsley, Gruyère, and Asiago. Bake for 12–15 minutes or until the top is brown and crisp. Serve while still bubbling.

Malfattini of Ricotta & Arugula with Pecorino & White Truffle Oil Sauce

2 tablespoons unsalted butter

6 ounces arugula, plus a few leaves to garnish

1¾ cups ricotta cheese, sieved

1 cup all-purpose flour

2 eggs

1 egg yolk

1 cup freshly grated Parmesan cheese, plus extra to serve

Freshly grated nutmeg

Salt & freshly ground black pepper

For the sauce

1¼ cups coarsely grated pecorino sardo cheese,

4 tablespoons unsalted butter

¼ cup mascarpone cheese

⅔ cup milk

2 tablespoons white truffle oil

The original recipe for these little gnocchi calls for sliced fresh Piedmont truffles—delicious but so expensive! Replace them with white truffle oil which is reasonably priced in comparison and available from specialty food shops. If you do happen to get hold of a white truffle, grate it over the top. Malfattini *means misshapen, which is appropriate as these are not the usual gnocchi shape. The sauce is a variation of the classic* fonduta *(see page 96), but uses pecorino instead of fontina.*

Heat the butter in a pan, add the arugula, and cook for 1 minute, until wilted. Let cool and then mince.

Put the ricotta, flour, eggs, and egg yolk in a bowl and mix well together. Stir in the Parmesan and arugula and season with nutmeg, salt, and pepper. Shape the mixture into ovals with 2 wet tablespoons, turning it between them. Drop them, in batches, into a large pan of lightly simmering salted water and cook until they rise to the surface. Remove with a slotted spoon and drain on paper towels. Keep them warm while you make the sauce.

Put the pecorino, butter, mascarpone, and milk in a bowl set over a pan of simmering water, making sure the water isn't touching the base of the bowl. Let the cheese melt slowly, whisking occasionally, then whisk in the truffle oil until the mixture comes together into a sauce. Season to taste.

To serve, warm the *malfattini* through in a low oven for a couple of minutes if necessary, then arrange them in serving bowls. Pour the sauce over, garnish with arugula, and sprinkle with a little extra Parmesan.

Chapter Five

Red Mullet on Baked Salad Caprese with Basil & Olive Oil

SERVES 4

2 balls of cow's milk mozzarella cheese, cut into slices ½ inch thick

8 plum tomatoes, skinned & cut into slices ½ inch thick

Salt & freshly ground black pepper

red mullet fillets, 6 ounces each, skin on

A small bunch of fresh basil

⅔ cup extra-virgin olive oil

A simple dish with fresh summer flavors. Caprese is the name given to the famous Italian salad of mozzarella, tomato, and basil. Here the tomato and cheese serve as a bed for red mullet, which is scattered liberally with fresh basil leaves. (See the photograph on page 2.)

Preheat the oven to 425°F. Lightly oil a shallow baking dish large enough to hold the red mullet fillets in a single layer. Arrange overlapping alternate slices of mozzarella and tomato on the bottom of the dish and season with salt and pepper. Lay the mullet fillets on top, skin-side up, season, scatter the basil leaves over, and pour on the olive oil. Bake for 8–10 minutes and then serve immediately.

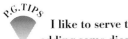

I like to serve this dish with some buttery noodles. Sometimes I vary it by adding some diced black olives to the pasta, or even a few sun-dried tomatoes.

Parmesan-Crusted Sea Bass with Thyme-Grilled Vegetables

SERVES 4

¾ cup freshly grated Parmesan cheese

½ cup fresh white bread crumbs

Grated zest of ½ lemon

Salt & freshly ground black pepper

4 sea bass fillets, 6 ounces each, skin on

2 eggs, beaten

¼ cup vegetable oil

2 tablespoons unsalted butter

For the vegetables

8 ounces zucchini, cut into slices ¼ inch thick (about 2 cups)

12 asparagus spears, peeled & well trimmed

2 cooked globe artichoke bottoms, cut into quarters

1 tablespoon fresh thyme leaves

¼ cup olive oil

2 tablespoons aged balsamic vinegar

Any firm fish would be suitable for this dish. You need to grill the vegetables with the thyme a day in advance and leave them overnight so that their juices run. The juices are then mixed with balsamic vinegar, making a delicious, thyme-scented vinaigrette to drizzle over the fish.

Put the zucchini, asparagus, and cooked artichokes in a roasting pan, season, sprinkle with the thyme leaves, and toss with the olive oil. Grill over charcoal (or cook under the broiler) for about 5–6 minutes, until the vegetables are slightly charred all over but still retain a bite. Leave overnight in the refrigerator, covered with plastic wrap.

The next day, drain the juices from the vegetables and reserve. Preheat the oven to 350°F.

Mix together the Parmesan, bread crumbs, lemon zest, and some seasoning. Season the bass fillets on both sides with salt and pepper. Put the beaten eggs in a shallow dish and dip the fish in them to coat both sides, then dip the fish in the Parmesan mixture, pressing it on well.

Reheat the grilled vegetables in the oven. Whisk 3 tablespoons of the reserved cooking juices with the balsamic vinegar.

Heat the oil and butter in a large frying pan until foaming, then add the Parmesan-coated fish fillets. Cook for about 3–4 minutes per side, until golden and crisp. To serve, arrange the thyme-grilled vegetables on serving plates, top with the bass, and drizzle the vinaigrette around.

P.G.TIPS For variation, rosemary and oregano could replace the thyme, while other good grilling vegetables, such as sweet peppers and eggplants, could be substituted for the zucchini, asparagus, and artichokes. Aged balsamic vinegar is best.

Saffron-Grilled Cod Fillet with Aligot & Beurre d'Escargot

SERVES 4

¼ cup olive oil

1 tablespoon lemon juice

¼ teaspoon saffron strands

cod fillets, 5 ounces each, skin on

1 quantity of freshly prepared Aligot (see page 135)

For the beurre d'escargot

10 tablespoons unsalted butter

2 garlic cloves, minced

3 tablespoons chopped fresh flat-leaf parsley, plus a few sprigs to garnish

¼ teaspoon Dijon mustard

2 tablespoons lemon juice

Salt & freshly ground black pepper

Beurre d'escargot tastes so good that it seems a shame to reserve it for serving just with snails. Here it is poured over grilled cod, served on a meltingly rich potato and cheese purée. The smell when it hits the table is something else! I like to accompany this dish with some haricot verte or grilled leeks.

Put the olive oil, lemon juice, and saffron in a pan and warm through to infuse the flavors. Pour this over the cod fillets and leave to marinate, either for 2 hours at room temperature or overnight in the refrigerator.

Next prepare the butter, which can be done well ahead of time. Melt the butter over a low heat, then add the garlic. Raise the heat a little and lightly fry the garlic without letting it color. Stir in the chopped parsley and mustard, then pour into a bowl and let cool. Add the lemon juice and season to taste.

To cook the cod, remove it from the marinade, season well, and place on a ridged cast-iron grill pan (or under the broiler). Cook until tender and golden, about 3–4 minutes per side on a grill pan or 5–6 minutes per side under the broiler. (You could also fry the fish.)

To serve, put a large dollop of aligot on each serving plate and top with the cod. Reheat the parsley and garlic butter and pour it over the fish, then garnish with sprigs of parsley.

P.G.TIPS Another way to serve the fish is to cook it lightly as usual, then to top it with a light mixture of fresh bread crumbs, mustard, and butter and brown it under the broiler before setting it down on the aligot.

Wing of Skate with Camembert, Spinach, Lardons & Cider

SERVES 4

4 ounces slab bacon, rind removed, cut in ¼-inch dice

2 cups button mushrooms, cut into ¼-inch dice

¼ cup crème fraîche

1 pound spinach, washed

½ small Camembert cheese, cut into ¼-inch dice

Salt & freshly ground black pepper

4 skate wings, 11 ounces each

4 pieces of *crépinette*, each about 10 inches square

3 tablespoons unsalted butter, chilled & diced, plus a little melted butter for brushing

5 tablespoons dry hard cider

⅔ cup dry white wine

⅔ cup Chicken Stock (see page 16)

2 tablespoons olive oil

1 tablespoon wholegrain mustard

ALTERNATIVE

CHEESE

Cooleeney, sometimes known as Irish Camembert

This dish calls for the skate to be enclosed in crépinette (caul fat), which seals in the filling and keeps the fish moist. A good butcher should be able to get it for you. You will need 4 very thin pieces.

Preheat the oven to 400°F. Heat a frying pan until smoking, add the bacon *lardons* and fry over a high heat until crisp. Add the mushrooms and fry for 2 minutes. Stir in the crème fraîche and cook until reduced by half. Then stir in the spinach, remove from the heat, and let cool. Add the diced Camembert and some seasoning.

Coat each skate wing with the Camembert and spinach mixture, spreading it evenly with a metal spatula. Brush the pieces of *crépinette* with melted butter, then put the skate on them, stuffing-side down. Wrap the fish well in the *crépinette* and put it in a baking dish large enough to hold it in a single layer. Pour the cider, wine, and chicken stock around the skate. Bake for 12–15 minutes, until tender. Remove the fish and keep warm. Strain the juices into a clean pan and whisk in the diced butter and olive oil a little at a time to form a sauce. Stir in the mustard and adjust the seasoning. Arrange the skate wings on a serving dish, pour over the sauce, and serve.

P.G. TIPS Other white-fleshed fish such as brill or turbot could replace the skate. Swiss chard or even finely shredded cabbage are good alternatives to the spinach.

Wine-Roasted Turbot on the Bone with Wilted Endive & Bleu d'Auvergne

SERVES 4

4 tablespoons unsalted butter, softened
3 ounces Bleu d'Auvergne cheese
2 tablespoons chopped fresh cilantro
¼ cup vegetable oil
Salt & freshly ground black pepper
Turbot steaks on the bone, 7 ounces each
⅔ cup dry white wine
⅔ cup Reduced Meat Stock (see page 17)

For the endive
2 heads Belgian endive
2 tablespoons unsalted butter
½ teaspoon sugar

For the salad
1 tablespoon walnut oil
2 tablespoons olive oil
1 tablespoon champagne vinegar
8 ounces corn salad (*mâche*)

ALTERNATIVE
CHEESES

Cashel Blue or Bleu des Causses

*F*ish and blue cheese are a rare combination, but I find they work surprisingly well here. Cooking fish on the bone is a useful technique that helps keep it moist and succulent.

Preheat the oven to 375°F. Beat the butter, Bleu d'Auvergne, and cilantro together and set aside.

Heat the oil in an ovenproof frying pan or a shallow flameproof casserole large enough to hold the fish in one layer. Season the turbot and fry in the oil for about 2 minutes on each side, until golden. Pour on the wine and stock, then place in the oven to bake for 10 minutes or until the fish is cooked through, basting it with the juices once or twice.

Meanwhile, remove the leaves from the Belgian endive, wash them, and cut them lengthwise into narrow strips. Put them in a pan with the butter and sugar and cook for 8–10 minutes, until all the liquid has evaporated and the endive is tender and lightly caramelized. Season to taste and keep warm.

For the salad, whisk together the oils and vinegar and season to taste, then toss with the corn salad.

Remove the fish from the oven; strain the juices into a pan and keep warm over a low heat. Keep the fish warm. Heat the cheese and cilantro butter in a frying pan until it is foaming and smells nutty. Add the foaming butter to the juices from the fish and season to taste. Arrange the endive on warm serving plates, top with the roasted turbot, and pour the sauce around. Serve immediately, accompanied by the salad.

P.G.TIPS　Belgian endive is most often found in salads nowadays, but it has a wonderful flavor if cooked gently in butter with a little sugar to offset the bitterness. Experiment by flavoring it with spices, and/or orange juice as well.

Stuffed Sardines with Parmesan Gremolata & Caper Butter

SERVES 4

24 fresh sardines, about 6 inches long, scaled

4 tablespoons olive oil

2 garlic cloves, minced

1 fennel bulb, with its green feathery leaves, minced

1 tablespoon chopped fresh thyme

1 tablespoon chopped fresh oregano

Grated zest of 1 lemon

1 tablespoon Pernod or other anise liqueur

½ cup fresh white bread crumbs

½ cup freshly-grated Parmesan cheese

Freshly grated nutmeg

Salt & freshly ground black pepper

For the caper butter

5 tablespoons unsalted butter

2 shallots, minced

3 tablespoons capers, rinsed & drained

1 tablespoon chopped fresh parsley

Juice of 1 lemon

ALTERNATIVE
CHEESES

Grana padana (a cheaper version of Parmesan), Asiago, or pecorino

Sardines have become newly fashionable over the past few years, and, what's more, they're good for us and very reasonably priced. This Parmesan, fennel, and lemon stuffing goes nicely with them. Mackerel can be used instead of sardines, if you prefer.

Preheat the oven to 400°F. Slit the sardines open along the belly and carefully pull out the entrails. Open the fish flat and carefully pull out the backbone from the head to the tail, snipping it off at the tail end with scissors and leaving the head and tail intact. Set the fish aside.

Heat half the oil in a pan, add the garlic, and cook gently until tender. Add the fennel and cook for 5 minutes. Then stir in the herbs, lemon zest, and Pernod, followed by the bread crumbs and Parmesan. Season to taste with nutmeg, salt, and pepper and remove from the heat.

Fill the cavity of each sardine with this mixture, pressing it in well. Put the fish on an oiled baking sheet, brush them with the remaining oil, and bake for 8–10 minutes, until cooked through.

For the caper butter, melt the butter over a low heat, then add the shallots, capers, and parsley. Cook until the butter begins to foam and becomes nutty in fragrance. Add the lemon juice, then immediately pour the butter over the sardines and serve.

Gratin of Lobster with Parmesan & Tarragon Sauce

SERVES 4

4 cooked lobsters, weighing about
1 pound each

2 tablespoons unsalted butter

Salt & freshly ground black pepper

Cayenne pepper, to taste

5 tablespoons dry white wine

1 tablespoon chopped fresh tarragon, plus
a few sprigs to garnish

1¼ cups Basic Cheese Sauce (see page 18)

¼ cup heavy cream, semi-whipped

3 (4) tablespoons freshly grated Parmesan
cheese

This is based on that great dish, lobster Thermidor. All you need to serve with it is a simple rice pilaff.

Cut the claws off the lobster with a large knife, then split the lobster in half down the back: The easiest way to do this is to put a large knife through the center of the body section and cut down through the head, then take out the knife, turn the lobster around, and cut down the center of the body through the tail. Remove and discard the head sac and the intestinal vein, then take out the lobster meat from the head and tail and cut it into large cubes. Discard the gills (known as "dead men's fingers") from the lobster shells and reserve the shells. Crack the claws in 2 or 3 places and pick out the meat.

Heat the butter in a pan, add the lobster meat, and season with salt, pepper, and cayenne. Pour in the white wine, bring to a boil, and simmer for 1 minute—no longer or the lobster will toughen. Remove the lobster from the pan with a slotted spoon and continue to boil the wine until it is reduced to half its original volume. Stir in the chopped tarragon and the cheese sauce, then fold in the cream. Return the lobster to the pan. Adjust the seasoning.

Fill the 8 lobster shells with the lobster mixture and put them on a baking sheet or in a shallow gratin dish. Sprinkle with the grated Parmesan. Brown under the broiler and then serve, garnished with sprigs of tarragon.

Sizzling Shrimp with Sofrito, Peppers & Manchego

SERVES 4

¼ cup olive oil

4 tablespoons unsalted butter

2 garlic cloves, minced

20–24 large shrimp, peeled & deveined

1 red onion, cut into wedges about ¼ inch thick

2 red sweet peppers, seeded & cut into strips ½ inch wide

1 green sweet pepper, seeded & cut into strips ½ inch wide

12 ounces tomatoes, skinned, seeded & chopped (about 1½ cups)

A pinch of cayenne pepper

½ teaspoon paprika

9 ounces Manchego cheese, cut into ¾-inch cubes (about 1 heaped cup)

Salt & freshly ground black pepper

2 tablespoons fresh cilantro leaves

ALTERNATIVE

CHEESE

Feta

Manchego is Spain's best-known cheese and, when fresh, has a mild, creamy consistency. Many Spanish recipes begin with instructions to prepare a sofrito— onions, garlic, tomatoes, and sometimes parsley, cooked slowly to make a thick, intensely flavored savory base. This particular dish is of Mexican-Spanish origin and could be made with almost any seafood. Try lobster or scallops for an extravagant version. Saffron rice makes a good accompaniment.

Heat the oil and butter in a frying pan until the butter is foaming, then add the garlic and cook for 1 minute. Throw in the shrimp and sauté them over a fairly high heat for about 1–2 minutes, until colored. Remove from the pan and keep warm. Add the onion and peppers to the pan, cover, and cook over a low heat for 15 minutes, until softened.

Stir in the tomatoes, cayenne, and paprika and cook for about 5 minutes, until the tomatoes begin to break down. Return the shrimp to the pan and stir together, then add the Manchego and sauté for 30 seconds. Season to taste, scatter the fresh cilantro over, and serve immediately.

Mussel Fondue Normandie

SERVES 6 as a first course, 4 as a main course

2 cups grated Emmenthal cheese

1 tablespoon cornstarch

½ garlic clove

1¼ cups dry white wine

9 ounces very ripe Camembert cheese, rind removed, cut into small pieces

6 tablespoons dry hard cider

Freshly grated nutmeg

Salt & freshly ground black pepper

For the mussels

2 pounds fresh mussels

1 shallot, minced

A few parsley stems

¾ cup dry white wine

I think that it's fair to say that most cheese dishes simply include a little cheese rather than use it as the main ingredient. One exception is fondue, a dish invented in the Swiss Alps to use the famous cheeses of the region, Emmenthal and Gruyère. My favorite fondue combines Emmenthal with Camembert from Normandy for a tasty modern variation. It is very important to have a proper fondue pot. This is easy to find and well worth a small investment in order to keep your fondue at the right temperature.

First clean the mussels. Scrub them under cold running water, pulling out their "beards" and scraping off any barnacles with a knife. Discard any open mussels that do not close when tapped lightly on a work surface.

For the fondue, gently toss the Emmenthal with the cornstarch and set aside. Rub the inside of a fondue pot or earthenware casserole with the cut surface of the garlic. Pour in the white wine and cook over a low heat until it just starts to bubble. Gradually stir in the Emmenthal and keep stirring until smooth. Then add the Camembert and blend together until the Camembert melts and the mixture is smooth again. Add the cider, and season with salt, pepper ,and nutmeg. Keep warm.

Place the mussels in a pan with the shallot, parsley stems and white wine. Cover with a tight-fitting lid and cook over a high heat, shaking the pan once or twice, until the mussels have opened (about 3–4 minutes). Drain them in a colander, reserving the cooking liquid, and discard any mussels that remain closed. Remove the mussels from their shells and keep warm. Strain the cooking liquid and add to the fondue. Serve the mussels with fondue forks to dip into the Camembert fondue.

P.G.TIPS **Any seafood would be good instead of mussels. I sometimes serve the fondue with new potatoes: Dip them into the pot too – delicious!**

Chicken Schnitzel with Mozzarella, Tomato Tapenade & Basil

SERVES 4

4 skinless boneless
chicken breast halves, 5 ounces each
Salt & freshly ground black pepper
Flour, for dusting
1 egg, beaten
¼ cup fresh white bread crumbs
¼ cup olive oil
½ cup unsalted butter
1 ball of mozzarella cheese,
cut into 8 slices
2 tablespoons roughly chopped fresh basil
Juice of ½ lemon

For the tomato tapenade
1½ cups sun-dried tomatoes
2½ tablespoons capers, rinsed & drained
2 garlic cloves, minced
¼ cup oil from the sun-dried tomatoes

The classic combination of mozzarella, tomato, and basil in a different guise. You can use turbot or a similar white fish instead of chicken and it works just as well. Tomato tapenade is now available in jars in many supermarkets, but I still think that homemade is better. Besides, it's really quick to make your own. You won't need to use all of it in this recipe, but it keeps well in the refrigerator.

For the tapenade, put all the ingredients in a blender and blitz unil course-fine (do not process it too finely, or it will become mushy).

Put the chicken breasts between 2 sheets of plastic wrap and beat lightly with a meat pounder or the end of a rolling pin until they are just under ¼ inch thick. Season with salt and pepper, then dust lightly with flour. Dip them in the beaten egg and then in the bread crumbs. Brush off any excess crumbs.

Heat the olive oil and 2 tablespoons of the butter in a frying pan and add the chicken. Cook for about 4–5 minutes on each side, until the chicken is golden and cooked through, then transfer to heatproof serving plates. Top each chicken breast with 2 slices of mozzarella, then spread ½ tablespoon of tomato tapenade over the cheese. Place under the broiler until the mozzarella begins to soften.

Meanwhile, heat the remaining butter in a frying pan until it is foaming and smells nutty. Add the basil and lemon juice. Pour the butter over the chicken and serve immediately.

P.G.TIPS
Sometimes I make this with tomato tapenade spread over one slice of mozzarella and black olive tapenade on the other. The contrast of black, red, and white looks spectacular. (Olive tapenade is available in jars in most supermarkets.)

Grilled Butterflied Chicken with Tomme, Ricotta Verde & Sweet Shallot Vinaigrette

SERVES 4

4 squab chickens or poussins,
about 1 pound each
Salt & freshly ground black pepper
3 ounces white Tomme cheese
scant ½ cup ricotta cheese
1 bunch of watercress, stems removed,
leaves minced
2 tablespoons chopped fresh basil
1 shallot, minced
1 garlic clove, minced
2 tablespoons olive oil
Lemon wedges, to serve

For the marinade
1 garlic clove, minced
Juice & grated zest of 2 lemons
¼ cup olive oil

For the vinaigrette
4 shallots, finely sliced
½ tablespoon unsalted butter
A pinch of sugar
1 tablespoon champagne vinegar
¼ cup olive oil
¼ teaspoon Dijon mustard

I recently discovered butterflied squab chickens in a major supermarket. What a superb idea! All the work has been done for you. If you are not lucky enough to find them, don't be too alarmed at the thought of preparing the birds yourself. After a few attempts you'll wonder what all the fuss was about. Your guests will be impressed too. Serve the chickens with a watercress salad and new potatoes.

To butterfly the chickens, you simply need to open them out flat. To do this, cut out the backbone with kitchen scissors or poultry shears. Break the wishbone, then turn each bird cut-side down and flatten it by pressing down with the heel of your hand. Turn it over and remove all the ribcage bones.

Mix together all the ingredients for the marinade, season with salt and pepper, and pour into a large shallow contain—you might need 2 to hold the chickens. Add the chickens, turning them to coat, then cover and let marinate for at least 4 hours, but preferably overnight, in the refrigerator.

To make the vinaigrette, gently fry the shallots in the butter with the sugar until golden and lightly caramelized. Whisk together the vinegar, oil, mustard, and some salt and pepper. Add the hot shallots and let cool. (This can be done several hours in advance.)

In a bowl, mix together the Tomme, ricotta, watercress, basil, shallot, garlic, and olive oil. Season to taste. Remove the chickens from the marinade and dry well. Carefully loosen the skin of each bird without detaching it and push the stuffing underneath, spreading it over the flesh—it's easiest to use your fingers. Smooth the skin over again and season with salt and pepper.

Grill the chickens over charcoal for about 7–8 minutes on each side, until tender and cooked through. Or, cook them on a ridged grill pan. Put them on warmed serving plates, drizzle a little of the vinaigrette over, and serve the rest on the side. Accompany with lemon wedges.

P.G.TIPS **If you find it difficult removing the ribcage from the raw chickens, take out the bones after the birds have been cooked. They will come away much more easily.**

GRILLED BUTTERFLIED
CHICKEN WITH TOMME,
RICOTTA VERDE & SWEET
SHALLOT VINAIGRETTE

Quails Stuffed with Sage Derby & Muscat Grapes

SERVES 4

8 quails, boned (ask your butcher to do this & give you the bones, if possible)

Salt & freshly ground black pepper

½ cup unsalted butter, softened

1 cup grated Sage Derby cheese

1 shallot, minced

1 small garlic clove, minced

For the sauce

⅓ cup white wine

1¼ cups Reduced Meat Stock (see page 17)

12 ounces muscat grapes

3 tablespoons Muscat de Beaumes de Venise or vin de Jura

ALTERNATIVE

CHEESES

Dolcelatte would be ideal. Even a stronger blue, such as Stilton or Roquefort, would work well.

This may seem rather an unusual combination, but, if you think about it, grapes are invariably served on a cheeseboard and they are also often cooked with quails. This recipe brings all three ingredients together. Muscat grapes are recommended for their exceptional sweetness, although the dish also works well with red grapes. Serve with artichoke bottoms or haricot verts that have been sautéed in butter with bacon and onions. If you cannot get hold of quails, you could use 4 squab chickens instead, in which case you would need to double the amount of stuffing.

Preheat the oven to 425°F. Season the quails inside and out. Prepare the stuffing by beating together 6 tablespoons of the butter, the Sage Derby, shallot, garlic, and a little seasoning. Stuff the quails with this mixture and seal them by pulling the skin over the opening and securing with a wooden toothpick. Place in a small roasting pan. Melt the remaining butter and brush it over the quails, then roast for 12–15 minutes, until juicy and tender and still slightly pink. Remove from the roasting pan and keep warm.

For the sauce, put the quail bones in the roasting pan, place it on a medium heat, and fry until the bones are golden brown. Add the white wine and bring to a boil, stirring to scrape up the sediment from the bottom of the pan. Simmer for 2 minutes, until the wine has evaporated. Pour in the meat stock and bring to a boil, skimming off any impurities from the surface. Reduce the heat and simmer for 10 minutes.

Meanwhile, pass half the grapes through a centrifugal juice extractor. When the sauce has reduced and thickened to a light, syrupy consistency, strain it through a sieve into a clean tin. Add the Beaumes de Venise or vin de Jura and the fresh grape juice. Simmer for 2 minutes, then add the remaining grapes to the sauce and reheat until boiling. Adjust the seasoning to taste.

Return the quails to the oven for 2 minutes to reheat them, then put them on 4 serving plates. Pour the sauce around the quails and serve.

P.G.TIPS **If you do not have a centrifugal juice extractor, purée the grapes in a blender, then sieve the purée. If seedless grapes are unavailable, remove seeds with a clean bobby pin or by cutting the grapes in half and removing the seeds.**

Roast Breast of Pheasant Wrapped in Bacon with Caraway Cabbage & Gorgonzola Polenta

SERVES 4

4 pheasant breasts, bones removed & chopped

Salt & freshly ground black pepper

8 bacon slices

4 tablespoons vegetable oil

6 tablespoons unsalted butter

1 head Savoy cabbage, central core removed, finely shredded

1 teaspoon caraway seeds

1¼ cups water

Freshly grated nutmeg

½ quantity of Gorzonzola Polenta (see page 132)

For the sauce

3 shallots, roughly chopped

1 garlic clove, roughly chopped

1 sprig of fresh thyme

1 bay leaf

6 juniper berries, lightly crushed

6 black peppercorns, lightly crushed

5 tablespoons red wine vinegar

⅔ cup red wine

⅔ cup Meat Stock (see page 17)

¼ cup port

½ tablespoon red-currant jelly

I often serve this winter-inspired dish around Christmas time, garnished with roasted baby onions and glazed chestnuts—delicious! Pheasant has a tendency to be dry if not cooked with care. By wrapping the breasts in bacon, you can keep them moist and tender.

Preheat the oven to 425°F. Season the pheasant breasts all over with salt and pepper, then wrap each one in 2 overlapping slices of bacon. Secure with a wooden toothpick. Heat half the oil and butter in an ovenproof frying pan or shallow casserole dish until foaming, then add the pheasant breasts and fry briefly until browned all over. Transfer to the oven and roast for 8–10 minutes, until tender.

Meanwhile, heat the remaining oil in a saucepan and cook the cabbage over a low heat until it begins to wilt. Add the remaining butter, the caraway seeds, and water. Bring to a boil and cook until the cabbage is tender and all the liquid has evaporated. Then season with salt, pepper, and a little nutmeg and keep warm.

Remove the pheasant breasts from the oven and take out the toothpicks. Keep the pheasant warm while you make the sauce. Put the chopped pheasant bones, shallots, garlic, thyme, bay leaf, juniper berries, and peppercorns in the pan in which the pheasant was cooked and fry gently for 2–3 minutes, until golden. Pour in the vinegar and boil for 1 minute, stirring to scrape up the sediment from the bottom of the pan. Add the red wine and boil until the liquid has reduced to half its original volume. Next add the stock and boil until reduced by a third. Stir in the port and red-currant jelly and adjust the seasoning. Strain through a fine sieve.

To serve, reheat the polenta if necessary. Arrange the cabbage on 4 warmed serving plates and place the pheasant on top. Garnish with a large scoop of polenta and pour the sauce around.

Grilled Steak Tartare with Roquefort

1¾ pounds ground round or sirloin
2 tablespoons Worcestershire sauce
1 onion, minced
1 tablespoon capers, rinsed,
drained & chopped
1 tablespoon chopped fresh parsley
1 tablespoon Dijon mustard
Salt & freshly ground black pepper
1 egg yolk
1 cup crumbled Roquefort cheese

ALTERNATIVE
CHEESES

For a different flavor entirely, substitute goat cheese or Emmenthal for the Roquefort.

This recipe sounds like a contradiction in terms, since the whole point of steak tartare is that it is served raw. But what I've done is taken the ingredients for steak tartare—best-quality ground beef, Worcestershire sauce, onions, capers, mustard, and egg yolk—and put them together into a hamburger, with the added bonus of delicious, melting Roquefort cheese in the center. Serve with good chunky fries and a crisp green salad.

Mix the beef, Worcestershire sauce, onion, capers, parsley, and mustard together in a bowl. Season with salt and pepper, then mix in the egg yolk. Chill for about 30 minutes, until firm.

Divide the mixture into 4 balls. With your thumb, make an indentation in each one and fill with the Roquefort. Pull the meat back over the cheese until it is completely covered. Flatten into hamburgers and season lightly. Grill over charcoal, or on a ridged cast-iron grill pan, or cook under the broiler.

Pepper-Crusted Rib-Eye Steaks with Roquefort Butter, Sautéed Potatoes & Porcini

SERVES 4

1 pound new potatoes

¼ cup olive oil

7 ounces fresh porcini (**Boletus edulis**), thinly sliced

2 tablespoons roughly chopped fresh sage

Salt and freshly ground black pepper

4 beef rib-eye steaks, about 10 ounces each, well trimmed

2 tablespoons coarsely ground black peppercorns

½ quantity of Roquefort Butter (see page 19)

This is a good dish for outdoor cooking, as it can be put together very easily. However, if it rains, you can always grill or fry the steaks indoors.

Cook the potatoes in boiling salted water until just tender, then drain and leave until cool enough to handle. Peel and cut into slices ½ inch thick. Heat the oil in a frying pan, add the potatoes, and sauté until golden and tender. Add the porcini and sage and sauté until the mushrooms are tender. Season with salt and pepper and keep warm.

Coat the rib-eye steaks evenly with the coarsely ground peppercorns and season with a little salt. Grill over charcoal until done to your liking.

Arrange the potatoes on 4 serving plates, top with the steaks, and put a pat of Roquefort butter on top of each steak. Serve immediately. The delicate cheese butter will melt on its way to the table.

P.G. TIPS

If you can't get fresh porcini mushrooms, use partobello mushrooms instead. This simple recipe lends itself to many adaptations—for instance, lamb or pork chops. The cheese butter is an ideal way to use up scraps of cheese.

Filet Mignon with Marrow & Parmesan Crostini & Red Wine–Balsamic Vinegar Jus

SERVES 4
....

4 filet mignons, 6 ounces each, well trimmed (cut the trimmings into small pieces & save for the sauce)

Salt & freshly ground black pepper

3 tablespoons vegetable oil

1 cup finely diced mixed vegetables, such as onion, leek & carrot

1 cup red wine

¼ cup aged balsamic vinegar

1¼ cup Reduced Meat Stock (see page 17)

8 large slices of beef bone marrow (see Tip)

4 round bread croûtes, 3 inches in diameter, toasted

1 ounce fresh Parmesan cheese, cut into shavings

ALTERNATIVE
....
CHEESE
....

Asiago

This dish evolved from the French classic, steak Bordelaise, which is beef in a red wine sauce with beef bone marrow. In my adaptation the marrow is topped with shaved Parmesan and the sauce enriched with aged balsamic vinegar. I generally serve it with buttered spinach with fresh porcini and pan-roasted shallots alongside, but any green vegetable would be good.

Season the steaks with salt and pepper. Heat the oil in a large heavy-based frying pan until smoking. Fry the steaks quickly on both sides so that they turn a beautiful rich dark color, then cook until they are done to your liking: 2–3 minutes each side for rare, 5–6 for medium. Remove from the pan and keep warm in a low oven. Add the meat trimmings to the pan, along with the mixed vegetables, and fry until golden. Pour in the red wine and balsamic vinegar and bring to a boil, stirring to scrape up the sediment from the bottom of the pan. Boil for 5 minutes, then pour in the stock and simmer until it has thickened slightly and become syrupy; it should be thick enough to coat the back of a spoon. Taste and adjust the seasoning if necessary.

Meanwhile, poach the slices of marrow in a little salted water, or, better still, meat stock, for 1 minute, then drain. Put 2 slices of poached marrow on each croûte and cover with the shaved Parmesan. Put the steaks on warm serving plates, top each one with a marrow crostini, and pour the red wine sauce around. Grind some black pepper over the top and serve.

P.G. TIPS

You will have to go to a good old-fashioned butcher's shop to get bone marrow. A very co-operative butcher might extract the marrow from the bone for you. If not, ask for bones cut into 3-inch lengths and then poach them for 1–2 minutes. This will enable you to scoop out the marrow easily.

Veal Steaks with Wisconsin Blue Cheese Rarebit, Roasted Celery Root & Rosemary Sauce

1½ pounds celery root, peeled and cut
into sticks 4 inches long and ¾ inch thick

⅓ cup vegetable oil

7 ounces Wisconsin blue cheese,
finely diced (about 1½ cups)

2 teaspoons Dijon mustard

½ cup light beer

Salt & freshly ground black pepper

4 veal tenderloin steaks,
about 5 ounces each, or veal chops

For the sauce
2 tablespoons unsalted butter

2 shallots, minced

1 tablespoon chopped fresh rosemary

⅔ cup red wine

2 cups Reduced Meat Stock (see page 17)

ALTERNATIVE
CHEESES

Any blue such as Stilton, Beenleigh Blue,
or Bleu des Causses.

A cheese rarebit is a peculiarly English dish that dates back at least to the time of Shakespeare. I came across this 18th-century recipe for blue cheese rarebit in an old cook book. I like to make it with one of my favorite cheeses, Scottish Dunsyre Blue.

Preheat the oven to 400°F. Blanch the celery root in boiling salted water for 2–3 minutes, then drain well in a colander. Place on a baking sheet, toss with half the oil, and bake for 20–25 minutes, until golden.

Meanwhile, for the rarebit, put the cheese, mustard, and beer in a pan over a low heat and cook, stirring constantly, until the cheese melts; the mixture should be the consistency of thickish cream. Season with pepper and keep warm.

Heat the remaining oil in a frying pan. Season the veal steaks and fry for about 3–5 minutes on each side. Remove from the pan and keep warm.

For the sauce, add the butter, shallots, and rosemary to the pan in which the veal was cooked and fry until the shallots are lightly golden. Pour in the red wine and boil for 2–3 minutes, then add the meat stock. Boil until reduced and thickened to a saucelike consistency, then strain through a fine sieve.

Spread the blue cheese rarebit over the veal steaks and place under the broiler for 2–3 minutes, until the rarebit has turned golden and bubbly. Transfer to serving plates, pour the sauce around, and garnish with the roasted celery root.

New-Look Saltimbocca

SERVES 4

4 veal scallops, 7 ounces each

Salt & freshly ground black pepper

4 slices of prosciutto

8 thin slices of fontina cheese,
rind removed

Flour, for dusting

3 eggs, beaten

¾ cup freshly grated Parmesan cheese

1 cup fresh white bread crumbs

¼ cup vegetable oil or clarified butter
(see Tip on page 83)

2 lemons, peel & pith removed, cut into
slices ¼ inch thick

For the sauce

1¼ cups Reduced Meat Stock
(see page 17)

¼ cup Marsala wine

6 tablespoons unsalted butter

20 small fresh sage leaves

2 tablespoons lemon juice

ALTERNATIVE
CHEESES

Port Salut or Fontal

My new-look saltimbocca uses all the elements of one of Italy's classic dishes, with the addition of thinly sliced fontina and a light Parmesan crust. In spring, asparagus tips and baby leeks make good accompaniments.

The veal scallops should be no more than ⅛ inch thick. If necessary, put them between 2 sheets of plastic wrap and flatten with a meat pounder or a rolling pin. Season the scallops with salt and pepper. Lay a slice of prosciutto on top of each one, then 2 slices of fontina. Fold up the edges of the veal to enclose the filling. Season again, then dust lightly with flour and chill for 30 minutes.

For the sauce, bring the stock and Marsala to a boil and simmer until it forms a light sauce consistency.

Beat together the eggs, Parmesan, and bread crumbs and add a little seasoning. Heat the oil or clarified butter in a large frying pan. Dip each veal scallop into the egg and cheese mixture to coat, then fry for about 5 minutes on each side, until golden and cooked through. Transfer to a warm serving dish. Top each scallop with 2 slices of lemon and pour the Marsala sauce around. Heat the butter until it is foaming and gives off a nutty aroma. Add the sage leaves and lemon juice and then pour over the veal. Serve immediately.

P.G.TIPS

It can be difficult judging the correct consistency of a sauce. If it seems too thin, reduce it by boiling until it has thickened enough to coat the back of a spoon.

Grilled Lamb Chops with Cilantro & Goat Cheese Pesto & Peppers

SERVES 4

⅓ cup olive oil

2 garlic cloves, minced

1 small hot red chili pepper

4 red sweet peppers, seeded

Salt & freshly ground black pepper

1 tablespoon white wine vinegar

8 thickly cut lamb rib chops

½ quantity of Cilantro & Goat Cheese Pesto (see page 20)

A creamy potato purée or some soft or grilled polenta would go well with the grilled lamb and sautéed red peppers in this dish.

Heat the olive oil in a frying pan, add the garlic and the whole chili, and cook for 1 minute over a low heat to infuse the oil. Cut the sweet peppers into strips ½ inch wide and add to the pan. Season with salt and pepper and sauté for 3–4 minutes. Add a little water, then cover and cook over a low heat for 10–15 minutes, until tender. Uncover the pan, raise the heat, and cook until all the liquid has evaporated. Add the vinegar and cook until that, too, has evaporated. Remove the chili and adjust the seasoning. Keep warm.

Season the lamb chops and grill them over charcoal or on a ridged cast-iron grill pan until they are done to your liking. Arrange the peppers on 4 serving plates, top with the lamb chops, spoon the pesto over, and serve.

Lamb Shanks with Feta, Anchovy & Braised Chickpeas

SERVES 6

1 tablespoon canned anchovy fillets, rinsed

2 tablespoons finely grated lemon zest

2 tablespoons chopped fresh oregano

¼ cup olive oil

2 garlic cloves, minced

6 small lamb shanks, trimmed

6 ounces Greek feta cheese

For the chickpeas

2 tablespoons olive oil

1 onion, minced

½ tablespoon ground cumin

1 teaspoon turmeric

1 heaped cup dried chickpeas, soaked overnight & then drained

4 tomatoes, skinned, seeded & chopped

Salt & freshly ground black pepper

1¼ cups tomato purée

Lamb shanks are always popular because they are tasty and very good value for money. Here they are served with Greek ingredients—oregano, feta, lemon, and olive oil—to make a hearty and satisfying dish.

For the chickpeas, heat the oil in a pan, add the onion, cumin, and turmeric, and sweat until the onion is tender. Add the chickpeas, cover with water, and bring to a boil. Reduce the heat and simmer for 1 hour, or until the chickpeas are tender. About 10 minutes before the end of cooking, add the chopped tomatoes and purée to form a thick sauce around the chickpeas. Season to taste.

Mince the anchovy fillets and mix with the lemon zest, oregano, oil, and garlic to make a paste. Rub the paste all over the lamb shanks. Leave to marinate for up to 2 hours at room temperature.

Grill the lamb over charcoal or a ridged cast-iron grill pan for 10–12 minutes on each side (this gives pink lamb), or until done to your liking.

Meanwhile, reheat the braised chickpeas and arrange on serving plates. Top with the lamb and coarsely grate the feta over the top. Serve immediately.

CHARGRILLED LAMB CHOPS
WITH CILANTRO & GOAT
CHEESE PESTO & PEPPERS

Chapter Six

Gratin of Leeks with Red Leicester & Bacon

SERVES 4

A pinch of sugar
8 medium leeks
1 tablespoo) unsalted butter
1 tablespoon all-purpose flour
1¼ cups Vegetable Stock (see page 16)
or low-fat milk
1 teaspoon Dijon mustard
⅓ cup heavy cream
1 cup grated Red Leicester cheese
Salt & freshly ground black pepper
2 ounces (2 slices) bacon,
coarsely chopped

Leeks and bacon make a wonderful marriage of flavors. With the addition of Red Leicester cheese, this simple gratin reaches new heights. It makes an ideal accompaniment to a good Sunday roast.

Bring a pan of water to a boil with the sugar and some salt. Plunge the leeks into the water and simmer for 8–10 minutes, until just tender. Remove and drain well, then dry on a cloth.

Melt the butter in a pan, stir in the flour, and cook over a gentle heat for 1–2 minutes. Gradually add the stock or milk and bring to a boil, stirring constantly. Reduce the heat and cook very gently for 10 minutes. Remove from the heat and stir in the mustard, cream, and half the cheese, then season to taste. Arrange the leeks in a gratin dish, season, and coat with the sauce.

In a hot frying pan, cook the bacon until crisp. Drain and scatter it over the leeks. Finally, sprinkle over the remaining cheese. Place under the broiler for a few minutes until bubbling and golden. Serve immediately.

Soft Gorgonzola Polenta with Young Spinach & Wild Mushrooms

SERVES 4–6

2 tablespoons unsalted butter

5 ounces mixed wild mushrooms, such as cépes or porcini, chanterelles & oyster mushrooms, halved if large

⅓ cup Madeira or port

1¼ cups Meat Stock (see page 17)

Salt & freshly ground black pepper

2 tablespoons olive oil

4 ounces young spinach leaves (about 1 cup), washed

Freshly grated nutmeg

1 tablespoon chopped fresh chives, to garnish

For the polenta

2 quarts water

2 teaspoons salt

½ cup unsalted butter

2 cups polenta flour

1 heaped cup crumbled Gorgonzola cheese

ALTERNATIVE CHEESES

Bleu de Bresse or Blue Castello (Australia)

I find this creamy blue cheese polenta far superior to the plain variety finished with Parmesan.

For the polenta, bring the water, salt, and butter to a boil in a large pan. Slowly rain in the polenta, stirring all the time. Simmer over a gentle heat for 30–35 minutes, stirring very frequently, until cooked; the polenta should be pulling away from the sides of the pan. Remove from the heat, stir in the Gorgonzola, and let it melt. The polenta should be quite soft and smooth in texture. Adjust the seasoning and keep warm.

Heat the butter in a pan and fry the wild mushrooms over a high heat until tender. Remove the mushrooms from the pan and set aside. Pour in the Madeira or port and stock and boil until the liquid has reduced by half. Season to taste. Return the mushrooms to the pan and keep warm.

Heat the olive oil in a pan, add the spinach, and cook until just wilted, then season with nutmeg, salt, and pepper.

To serve, pour the polenta into 4 warmed shallow bowls, place the spinach in the center, and arrange the mushrooms on top. Garnish with the chives.

Eggplant & Oregon Blue Soufflé

SERVES 6

2 tablespoons freshly grated
Parmesan cheese

½ cup olive oil

3 medium eggplants, peeled & cut into
small cubes

⅔ cup water

Salt & freshly ground black pepper

A large pinch of paprika

3 ounces Oegon Blue cheese, crumbled
(about ½ cup)

3 tablespoons unsalted butter,
plus extra for greasing

¼ cup all-purpose flour

1 cup milk, boiled
& strained

4 egg yolks

6 egg whites

ALTERNATIVE
CHEESES

Bleu d'Auvergne, Lanark Blue, Roquefort
or Meredith Blue (Australia)

Some people find the idea of cooking a soufflé too daunting to contemplate, but as long as you follow the rules it can be a very simple dish to add to your repertoire. Here is one of my personal favorites. A delicious variation for any cheese soufflé is to put some diced cheese in the center of the mixture when you are filling the dish. It will melt as the soufflé cooks, resulting in a wonderful fondue-like texture.

Butter six 1-cup soufflé dishes or one 5-cup soufflé dish and dust them with the Parmesan, turning the dishes to coat them evenly. Tip out any excess cheese.

Preheat the oven to 450°F. Heat the olive oil in a large frying pan, add the eggplants, and fry until lightly golden. Don't crowd the pan: You may have to cook them in batches. Return all the eggplants to the pan, add the water, cover, and cook over a gentle heat for up to 30 minutes, stirring occasionally, until the eggplants are very soft and fairly dry in texture. Put them in a blender with a little salt, some pepper, and the paprika. To this add ¼ cup of the Oregon Blue and blitz to a smooth, thickish purée. Set aside.

Heat the butter in a pan, add the flour, and cook over a low heat for a few minutes. Gradually add the hot milk, stirring all the time, then bring to a boil to make a smooth sauce. Cook over a very low heat for about 5 minutes, then stir in the eggplant and Oregon Blue purée. Let cool slightly before stirring in the egg yolks.

Whisk the egg whites until they form stiff peaks. Beat a third of the whites into the sauce to loosen the mixture, then carefully fold in the remaining whites. Half fill the soufflé dishes with the mixture and scatter the remaining Oregon Blue over the top. Pour over the remaining soufflé mixture and wipe any drips off the rims of the dishes. Place on a baking sheet and bake for 20 minutes, until all the soufflés are well risen and nicely golden. Serve immediately.

P.G.TIPS For successful soufflé making: ● Ensure that the bowl in which you whisk the egg whites is clean and greasefree; rub it with a little lemon, then rinse under cold water and dry with a clean cloth ● Do not overbeat the egg whites or they will become grainy ● Be careful not to leave fingerprints along the rim of the soufflé dish or the soufflé will not rise evenly ● Soufflés must be served immediately. Remember: "The guests should wait for the soufflé and not the other way around!"

Aligot
(Cheese & Potato Purée)

SERVES 4

2 pounds boiling potatoes

¾ cup milk, boiled & strained

5 tablespoons heavy cream or
crème fraîche

4 tablespoons unsalted butter

4 ounces (4 slices) bacon, diced

Salt & freshly ground black pepper

1 pound full-fat Tomme cheese,
such as Cantal, cut into thin slivers

ALTERNATIVE
CHEESES

Although Cantal is the usual cheese,
Gruyère, Emmenthal, fontina, and even
Lancashire all make good substitutes.

*Aligot is a peasant dish from the Auvergne region of France and makes
hearty and sustaining cold-weather fare. In some areas garlic is traditionally
included. It's very good served with sausages, braised meat, or even, less
conventionally, with fish—see the recipe for Saffron-Grilled Cod Fillet with
Aligot and Beurre d'Escargot on page 104.*

Peel the potatoes and cook them in boiling salted water until tender. Drain
well and mash until very smooth, then beat in the milk, cream or crème
fraîche, and butter.

In a separate pan, cook the bacon until it is crisp and the fat has been
released. Add the fat (not the bacon itself) to the potato purée and season to
taste. Place over a low heat and gradually fold in the cheese using a spatula.
Beat the mixture; as it becomes elastic it will soften slightly and eventually be
stringy when lifted with the spoon. As soon as it reaches this stage, you
should serve the dish immediately.

P.G.TIPS

Aligot loses its heat fairly quickly, so your guests must be ready to eat it at once
to appreciate it at its best. Vegetarians can omit the bacon fat.

Involtini di Melanzane al Formaggio

SERVES 4

Olive oil, for frying

2 large eggplants, cut lengthwise into slices ¼ inch thick

⅔ cup tomato purée

1 ball of buffalo mozzarella cheese, cut into slices ¼ inch thick

For the stuffing

4 ounces provolone cheese, cut into small cubes (about ¾ cup)

½ heaped cup pine nuts

⅓ cup raisins, soaked in water until plump, then drained

¼ cup olive oil

2 tablespoons fresh white bread crumbs

1 garlic clove, minced

2 tablespoons freshly grated Parmesan cheese

1 tablespoon chopped fresh basil

Salt & freshly ground black pepper

1 egg, beaten

In my adaptation of this classic Italian dish from Campania, the eggplant slices are rolled up with a cheese, basil, and raisin stuffing rather than layered in the usual way. It makes a delicious and substantial vegetarian main course.

Preheat the oven to 375°F. Heat a generous quantity of olive oil in a frying pan and fry the eggplant slices, a few at a time, until golden on both sides, adding more oil if necessary. Drain on paper towels and let cool.

For the stuffing, mix together the provolone, pine nuts, raisins, olive oil, bread crumbs, garlic, Parmesan, and basil. Season to taste and bind together with the egg. Lay out the cooked eggplant slices on a work surface and divide the stuffing among them. Roll them up fairly tightly to secure the filling and season with salt and pepper. Lightly grease a gratin dish with a little olive oil and put the eggplant rolls in it, packing them in tightly. Pour the tomato purée over and arrange the mozzarella slices down the center. Drizzle with a little more olive oil and grind some salt and pepper over. Bake for 25–30 minutes, until golden. Cool slightly before serving.

P.G.TIPS **Although this is usually eaten hot, I was once served it cold by an Italian friend whose mother swore that it tasted better cold the next day. You know, I think I have to agree with her. Why not try it, and judge for yourself?**

Zuccini & Cheddar Clafoutis with Rosemary

SERVES 4

2 tablespoons all-purpose flour

3 eggs

2 cups milk

12 ounces zucchini, or half zucchini and half yellow summer squash, cut into slices ½ inch thick

Salt & freshly ground black pepper

1 garlic clove, minced

1 tablespoon chopped fresh rosemary, plus a few leaves to garnish

5 ounces Cheddar cheese, thinly sliced

Many people have rosemary bushes growing in their garden but only ever think to put this herb with lamb. Try it in this vegetarian dish and you'll find it partners the zucchini surprisingly well. I suggest you serve the clafoutis as a light main course.

Preheat the oven to 400°F. Beat the flour, eggs, and milk together to make a smooth batter (or whizz them in a blender). Let stand for 20 minutes. Cook the zucchini in boiling salted water for 30 seconds, then drain well and dry them. Arrange them in overlapping circles on the bottom of a buttered 9-inch gratin dish or flan dish and then season with salt and pepper.

Stir the garlic and chopped rosemary into the batter and pour it over the zucchini Lay the cheese slices on top, scatter over a few rosemary leaves, and bake for 30–35 minutes, until golden and well puffed up. Serve warm rather than hot. The *clafoutis* will sink before serving, so don't be alarmed.

P.G.TIPS **This recipe makes a good blueprint for all sorts of variations. Try substituting butternut squash for the zucchini or mushrooms that have been lightly sautéed with garlic, or even a combination of winter squash and mushrooms.**

Winter Vegetable Pan Haggerty

SERVES 4

¼ cup vegetable oil

1 onion, thinly sliced

7 ounces rutabaga, cut into fine matchsticks or coarsely grated (about 1½ cups)

7 ounces turnips, cut into fine matchsticks or coarsely grated (about 1½ cups)

7 ounces potatoes, cut into fine matchsticks or coarsely grated (about 1½ cups)

6 tablespoons unsalted butter, melted

Salt & freshly ground black pepper

¾ cup grated Cheddar cheese

ALTERNATIVE
CHEESES

Isle of Mull or mild Parmesan

Pan Haggerty originates from Northumbria, England, and is normally just potatoes, onions, and cheese layered in a frying pan and cooked on top of the stove. My version uses a selection of root vegetables for color and flavor and is baked in the oven rather than fried. It's good served with ham, but also makes a very nice vegetarian dish.

Preheat the oven to 400°F. Heat the oil in a flameproof gratin dish, add the onion, and cook for 1–2 minutes, until the onions are softened, but not colored.

Drain the root vegetables separately in a colander to remove any excess moisture, then pat dry. Place a layer of rutabaga over the onion, brush well with melted butter, season, and then sprinkle on some grated cheese. Top with the turnips and more Cheddar, seasoning them and brushing with butter as before. Finally, top with the potatoes, season, and butter well. Add a final layer of cheese, then transfer to the oven and bake for about 45 minutes, until cooked through and lightly golden.

Turnips Stuffed with Mascarpone Creamed Spinach & Beaufort Cheese

SERVES 4

4 round turnips, about 3 inches in diameter, peeled

Salt & freshly ground black pepper

4 tablespoons unsalted butter

1 pound fresh spinach

¼ cup heavy cream

¼ cup mascarpone cheese

Freshly grated nutmeg

¾ cup grated Beaufort cheese

**ALTERNATIVE
CHEESES**

Cheddar, Cantal, or Gruyère

I love these simple cheese-stuffed turnips. Mascarpone is extremely rich but very good, although the first time I made the turnips I used a creamed Gorgonzola mixture. That is just as good, but, like a true chef, I enjoy experimenting with many variations. I usually serve the turnips with roast lamb, which is wonderful. Try using this stuffing in other vegetables, such as tomatoes, baby summer squash, or artichokes.

Preheat the oven to 375°F. Cook the whole turnips in boiling salted water until just tender. Drain and let cool, then cut them in half horizontally. With a spoon, carefully scoop out the centers, taking great care to leave the sides of the turnips intact. Season the inside with salt and pepper.

Heat the butter in a frying pan, add the spinach, and cook for 3–4 minutes, until it has wilted and become tender. Stir in the cream and mascarpone and season with nutmeg, salt, and pepper. Fill the turnip halves with this mixture.

Place the turnip halves in a baking dish and sprinkle the grated Beaufort over. Bake for 10–12 minutes, or until the cheese is browned, then serve.

Herb-Cheese Sausages

SERVES 4

1½ cups grated Cheshire cheese

4½ cups fresh white bread crumbs,
plus 2–2½ cups for coating

2 scallions or small leeks, minced

1 teaspoon mustard powder

1 teaspoon fresh thyme leaves

1 teaspoon chopped fresh rosemary

Freshly grated nutmeg

Salt & freshly ground black pepper

2 eggs, separated

Flour, for dusting

Vegetable oil, for deep- or shallow-frying

ALTERNATIVE
CHEESES

Caerphilly, Cheddar, or Cornish Yarg

These meatless sausages from Wales are also known as Glamorgan sausages and are usually made with Caerphilly or Cheddar cheese and leeks. My favorite version uses Kirkham's Lancashire or sometimes Cornish Yarg. Serve the sausages with a tomato sauce or chutney.

Mix together the cheese, bread crumbs, scallions or leeks, mustard, and herbs. Season with nutmeg, salt, and pepper, then add the egg yolks and knead well to form a soft paste that holds its shape. Chill to firm the mixture slightly, then shape it into 12 sausages.

Whisk the egg whites just until frothy. Dust the sausages in flour, then dip them in the egg whites, and, finally, roll them in bread crumbs until thoroughly coated. Deep- or shallow-fry the sausages for 3–4 minutes, or until golden, turning them occasionally. Drain on paper towels and serve.

Lancashire Cheese, Onion & Corn Pudding

SERVES 4

4 tablespoons unsalted butter, plus extra
for greasing

1 onion, minced

1 large ear corn

1½ cups milk

⅓ cup all-purpose flour

½ teaspoon Dijon mustard

1 heaped cup Lancashire cheese, grated

Freshly grated nutmeg

Salt & freshly ground black pepper

4 eggs, separated

For the sauce

½ cup Vegetable Stock (see page 16)

4 tablespoons unsalted butter,
chilled & diced

2 tomatoes, skinned, seeded & chopped

½ cup fava or lima beans, cooked

10 fresh basil leaves, shredded

ALTERNATIVE

CHEESES

Wensleydale or Caerphilly

This is more of a "pudding soufflé" than a heavy pudding. Softer and quicker to ripen than Cheddar, Lancashire is the ultimate toasting cheese. Kirkham's Lancashire is the very best and, although it is usually served only on good cheeseboards, I find it hard to resist using it in cooking, too.

Preheat the oven to 350°F. Heat 2 tablespoons of the butter in a heavy-based pan, add the onion, cover, and sweat until tender. Shuck the corn, then cut off the kernels. Add them to the onion and sweat for 5 minutes, until soft. Meanwhile, chop the corn cob into small pieces and place in a pan with the milk. Bring to a boil and simmer for 5 minutes to infuse the milk, then strain.

When the corn and onion are cooked, remove from the pan. Set aside 1 tablespoon of the corn kernels to use in the sauce. Add the remaining butter to the pan, sprinkle in the flour, and stir for 1–2 minutes to form a *roux*. Pour the infused milk onto the *roux* a little at a time, blending it in well and stirring constantly to make a thick sauce. Stir in the mustard, cheese, onion, and corn and season to taste with nutmeg, salt, and pepper. Remove from the heat and cool slightly, then beat in the egg yolks.

Whisk the egg whites until stiff enough to hold their shape. Beat a third of the whites into the corn and cheese mixture, then gently fold in the remaining whites.

Lightly butter four 1-cup soufflé dishes and fill them two-thirds full with the mixture. Place in a roasting pan containing enough hot water to come at least halfway up the sides of the dishes. Bake for 20 minutes, until risen and lightly set.

Meanwhile, make the sauce. Bring the stock to a boil in a small pan and boil for 2 minutes. Remove from the heat and whisk in the chilled butter, a few pieces at a time, to form an emulsion. Stir in the tomatoes, fava beans, reserved corn kernels, and basil. Season to taste with salt and pepper.

When the puddings are done, cool them slightly before unmolding them onto serving plates. Pour the sauce around and serve immediately.

P.G.TIPS **I find that eggs that are about 1 week old are best for soufflés. I've no idea why! Don't let the cheese and corn mixture become completely cold before adding the beaten egg whites, or the puddings will not rise to their full extent.**

Potato Cakes with Ricotta & Chives

SERVES 4

1½ pounds potatoes

4 tablespoons unsalted butter

2 shallots, minced

½ cup all-purpose flour

1 egg

1 egg yolk

⅓ cup firm ricotta cheese

2 tablespoons chopped fresh chives

Freshly grated nutmeg

Salt & freshly ground black pepper

3 tablespoons clarified butter (see Tip on page 83) or vegetable oil

ALTERNATIVE

CHEESES

Fresh goat cheese or a grated hard cheese

A simple but great-tasting vegetable dish to serve with meat or fish, or even as a breakfast accompaniment. Try the potato cakes for brunch, topped with a poached egg and Hollandaise sauce as a variation on eggs Benedict.

Cook the potatoes in their skins in simmering salted water until tender, then drain well. Peel and press through a potato ricer or sieve while still hot; you will need 2 cups potato purée. Heat the butter in a pan, add the shallots, and sweat until tender but not colored. Stir in the flour to make a thick *roux* and cook for 1 minute over a low heat. Remove from the heat. Beat in the egg and egg yolk and then beat in the potato purée, ricotta, and chives. Season with nutmeg, salt and pepper and then leave to cool.

Shape the mixture into 8 potato cakes and fry in the clarified butter or oil for 4–5 minutes on each side, until golden. Serve immediately.

P.G.TIPS

You can use the potato cake mixture to make delicious gnocchi, by rolling it into small balls and poaching them in boiling salted water. Put them in a gratin dish, pour a richly flavored tomato sauce on top, and sprinkle them with grated Parmesan or Cheddar cheese. Then brown the gnocchi under the broiler.

Goat Cheese & Parsley Mash

SERVES 4

1¾ pounds potatoes, peeled & cut
into chunks

1 cup milk, warmed

4 tablespoons unsalted butter, softened

4 ounces soft goat cheese such as
Roubiliac, pressed through a sieve
(about ½ cup)

2 tablespoons chopped fresh
flat-leaf parsley

Freshly grated nutmeg

Salt & freshly ground black pepper

This potato and cheese mash is particularly good served with roast or grilled chicken or lamb.

Put the potatoes in a pan of cold salted water and bring to a boil, then simmer until tender. Drain the potatoes and, while still hot, put them through a potato ricer or mash well.

Beat in the warm milk and the butter, then fold in the sieved goat cheese and parsley. Season with nutmeg, salt, and pepper and serve immediately.

Rutabaga Mash with Cheddar & Black Pepper Butter

SERVES 4

1½ pounds rutabaga, peeled & cut into
small cubes

2 tablespoons olive oil

¼ cup milk

1 cup mild grated mild Cheddar cheese

5 tablespoons unsalted butter

Salt

1 teaspoon cracked black pepper
(see Tip)

Rutabaga is, sadly, rather unpopular, yet in the right hands it can be one of the most flavorful vegetables. Potato mashes are currently very fashionable, but perhaps rutabaga mash is the one to watch for the future! This recipe is also good when made with parsnips.

Cook the rutabaga in boiling salted water until tender, then drain well. Purée in a blender with the oil and milk until smooth. Transfer to a clean pan and heat through, then beat in the Cheddar and 1 tablespoon of the butter. Season with salt to taste, then transfer to a warmed serving dish.

Melt the remaining butter with the cracked black pepper, pour it over the purée, and serve immediately.

P.G. TIPS
To make cracked black pepper, put some peppercorns in a small bowl and break them up roughly with the end of a rolling pin, or use a pestle and mortar.

RUTABAGA MASH
WITH CHEDDAR &
BLACK PEPPER BUTTER

Chapter Seven

Sambuca-Flamed Ricotta with Chilled Summer Berries

SERVES 4

1 cup firm ricotta cheese

¼ cup sugar, or to taste

½ cup Sambuca

½ cup heavy cream, semi-whipped

1½–2 cups mixed berries, such as raspberries, strawberries & red currants, chilled

3 ounces white chocolate, cut into shavings (optional)

Sambuca is an Italian anise liqueur. If you don't have any, you could use a fruit brandy or ordinary brandy instead. This easy dessert makes a great finale to a barbecue.

Beat the ricotta, sugar, and 3 tablespoons of the Sambuca together until creamy. Gently fold in the whipped cream and transfer to a serving bowl. Chill for at least 4 hours.

Just before serving, heat the remaining Sambuca in a small pan until very hot and pour it over the ricotta mixture. Ignite with a match; then, when the flames have died down, top with the chilled summer berries. Finish with the white chocolate shavings, if using, and serve immediately.

P.G. TIPS

Try serving this with a fresh berry *coulis* on the side. The addition of a few toasted, sliced almonds and a little sprig of mint makes an attractive decoration and alternative to the chocolate shavings.

Rhubarb in Chilled Punch Syrup with Cheese Sorbet

SERVES 4

1½ cups red wine

¼ cup grenadine syrup

Juice & grated zest of 1 orange

1 cinnamon stick

½ cup sugar

1¾ pounds rhubarb, peeled & cut into
2-inch lengths (about 7 cups)

For the cheese sorbet

2¼ cups milk

scant 1 cup sugar

Juice & grated zest of 1 small orange

¾ cup cream cheese

For an interesting contrast, you could serve the rhubarb and punch syrup with the sorbet while they are still warm.

For the sorbet, put the milk, sugar, and orange juice and zest in a pan and bring to a boil, stirring to dissolve the sugar. Remove from the heat and let cool, then stir this mixture into the cream cheese. Pour into an ice cream machine and freeze until firm, following the manufacturer's instructions.

If you don't have an ice cream machine, pour the mixture into a shallow container and put it in the freezer. After about 30 minutes, when the mixture is beginning to set, remove from the freezer and beat well with an electric mixer or whisk to disperse any ice crystals, then return it to the freezer. Repeat this 2 or 3 times and then freeze until firm.

For the punch syrup, put the wine, grenadine syrup, orange juice and zest, cinnamon and sugar into a pan and boil until reduced to half its original volume. Add the rhubarb to the syrup and cook gently for up to 5 minutes, until the rhubarb is tender and sweet but still holds its shape. Transfer to a bowl and let cool, then chill thoroughly. Serve with scoops of the cheese sorbet.

My Favorite Pick-Me-Up

S E R V E S 4

2 eggs

⅓ cup sugar

2 tablespoons Kahlua liqueur

½ cup mascarpone cheese

½ cup heavy cream, semi-whipped

⅓ cup strong espresso coffee

8 lady fingers or savoiardi, cut into
½-inch cubes

1 orange, all peel and pith removed,
divided into sections, to decorate

For the orange sauce
½ cup sugar

Juice of 2 large oranges

Grated zest of 1 large orange

2 tablespoons Grand Marnier

This is, in fact, a frozen version of that astonishingly popular dessert, tiramisù, *which means "pick-me-up" in Italian. It is served with a refreshing orange sauce, but a plain coffee or even chocolate sauce would also be extremely good.*

Put the eggs, sugar, and Kahlua in a bowl set over a pan of simmering water, making sure the water is not touching the base of the bowl. Whisk until the mixture is pale, thick, and creamy and has doubled in volume; a portable electric mixer is useful for this. Remove the bowl from the pan of water and continue to whisk until the mixture is cold.

Warm the mascarpone slightly, then fold it gently but thoroughly into the mousse mixture, making sure there are no lumps. Next, gently fold in the whipped cream.

Put the espresso coffee in a shallow bowl and soak the lady finger cubes in it for 1 minute. Take 4 metal rings, each 2½ inches in diameter and 2 inches high, and place them on a baking sheet. Layer the lady fingers and mascarpone cream in the rings until they are full, then smooth the tops with a metal spatula. Place in the freezer for at least 3 hours, preferably overnight.

To make the orange sauce, melt the sugar in a heavy-based pan over a medium heat and stir constantly until it forms a light caramel. Carefully add the orange juice—it may splutter at first—and the zest. At this stage the mixture will crystallize; reduce the heat and cook for 2–3 minutes and the sugar will liquefy again. Stir in the Grand Marnier, then strain the sauce. Let cool and then chill until ready to use.

To serve, unmold the frozen *tiramisù* onto individual serving plates and pour the sauce around. Decorate with the orange sections.

P.G.TIPS

If you don't have any metal rings you could use ramekins, although the *tiramisù* won't look as neat when unmolded. In an emergency it is not unknown for chefs to use clean plastic guttering, cut into appropriate lengths!

Goat Cheese Mousse with Pineapple Confit

SERVES 6–8

1 small pineapple

1 cup granulated sugar

1¼ cups water

1½ pounds mild fresh goat cheese, such as Sainte-Maure or Roubiliac

1¾ cups confectioners' sugar

1 cup heavy cream, semi-whipped

For the black-currant sauce

2 cups fresh or frozen black currants, plus extra to decorate

Juice of 1 orange

A little sugar, to taste

This dessert first appeared in my book Virtually Vegetarian, *but it has proved so popular and makes such good use of goat cheese that I felt I had to include it here as well.*

Remove the skin of the pineapple and cut the flesh into rings, then remove the hard central core. Put the granulated sugar and water in a pan and heat gently to dissolve the sugar, then bring to a boil to make a syrup. Add the pineapple, reduce the heat, and simmer gently for about 45 minutes, until the pineapple becomes tacky and candied in appearance. Let cool in the syrup. (This can be made in advance and keeps well in the refrigerator.)

Put the goat cheese and confectioners' sugar in a food processor and process until smooth, then transfer to a bowl. Drain the pineapple well and let it dry, then cut it into very small dice and add to the cheese. Gently fold in the whipped cream. Place the mixture in the refrigerator to firm up for at least 4 hours, or overnight.

For the sauce, put the black currants in a blender with the orange juice and sugar and blitz to a smooth purée. Strain through a fine sieve.

Either serve the mousse in a single large glass bowl and pass the black-currant sauce separately, or shape the mousse into quenelles (ovals) with 2 tablespoons, arrange them on serving plates, and pour the sauce around. Decorate with black currants.

Goat Cheese Ice Cream

2¼ cups milk

½ cup heavy cream

4 egg yolks

1 egg

½ cup sugar

4½ ounces mild soft goat's cheese,
such as Sainte-Maure or
mild Ribblesdale

You may be surprised to see goat cheese in an ice cream but it gives it a delicious tanginess. The ice-cream makes a wonderful foil for cherries—try it with a warm cherry tart or clafoutis. I have included instructions for freezing without an ice cream machine, though I believe that for fine-textured ice creams and sorbets you do need to invest in a machine. They are quite reasonably priced now and once you have one the possibilities are endless.

Bring the milk and cream to a boil. Whisk the egg yolks, whole egg and sugar together until thick, pale, and creamy. Pour the milk and cream slowly onto the eggs, whisking all the time. Return the mixture to the pan and stir with a wooden spoon over a gentle heat until the custard has thickened enough to coat the back of the spoon. Do not let it boil or the eggs will scramble. Remove from the heat and stir in the cheese until it has melted into the custard. Strain through a fine sieve and let cool.

Pour the mixture into an ice cream machine and freeze according to the manufacturer's instructions. If you don't have an ice cream machine, pour the custard into a shallow container and place it in the freezer. After about 30 minutes, when it is beginning to set, remove it from the freezer and beat with an electric mixer or whisk to disperse any ice crystals, then return it to the freezer. Repeat 2 or 3 times and then freeze until firm.

Brie Ice Cream with Dates, Walnuts & Butterscotch Sauce

SERVES 8

Ingredients for the Goat Cheese Ice Cream (above), replacing the goat cheese with semi-ripe Brie cheese

1 cup dates, pitted & cut into strips

2 tablespoons walnuts in large pieces

For the butterscotch sauce

½ cup light brown sugar

⅓ cup heavy cream

6 tablespoons unsalted butter

½ teaspoon vanilla extract

This is a shamelessly indulgent confection, rich and sticky and quite irresistible. Make sure you buy the very best quality dates, such as the succulent Medjool variety, in order to do it justice.

Remove the rind from the Brie and cut the cheese into small pieces. Make the ice cream as for the Goat Cheese Ice Cream and freeze until firm.

For the sauce, put all the ingredients in a heavy-based saucepan and cook over a medium heat for 3–5 minutes, stirring all the time, until the color changes to a light caramel. Let cool and then chill.

To serve, put scoops of ice cream in glass *coupes* and scatter the dates and walnuts over. Lightly coat with the chilled butterscotch sauce.

BRIE ICE CREAM WITH
DATES, WALNUTS &
BUTTERSCOTCH SAUCE

Panna "Ri-cotta"

SERVES 4

¼ cup milk

⅔ cup heavy cream

½ cup sugar

Grated zest of ½ orange

½ cup freshly made strong coffee,
preferably espresso

½ vanilla bean, split

2 gelatin leaves

2 tablespoons rum

1 cup firm ricotta cheese, pressed
through a sieve

Sprigs of fresh mint, to decorate
(optional)

For the apricot compote

½ cup sugar

⅓ cup water

Juice of ½ lemon

12 ounces fresh apricots, pitted & sliced

Panna cotta, *meaning "cooked cream," is a traditional Piedmontese pudding of molded cream lightly set with gelatin. Unconventionally, this recipe includes ricotta, so I have christened it Panna "Ri-cotta." Moving even farther away from tradition, it is flavored with coffee and served with a fresh apricot compote.*

Put the milk, cream, sugar, and orange zest in a pan and bring to a boil. Stir in the coffee and scrape in the seeds from the vanilla bean, then add the bean as well. Remove from the heat and let cool. Meanwhile, put the gelatin in a small pan, cover with cold water, and let soak for 5 minutes. Heat gently until the gelatin has melted.

Take the vanilla bean out of the pan and stir in the rum, sieved ricotta, and the gelatin. Strain through a fine sieve, then pour into 4 ramekins or similar molds and chill for at least 2 hours, until set.

For the compote, put the sugar, water, and lemon juice in a pan and bring slowly to a boil, stirring to dissolve the sugar. Reduce the heat, add the sliced apricots, and poach for about 5 minutes, until just tender. Remove from the heat and let cool, then chill.

Unmold the coffee ricotta custards, or serve them in the ramekins if you prefer, accompanied by the apricot compote and decorated with sprigs of mint, if desired.

Crunchy Quark Pavlovas with Caramelized Pineapple

SERVES 6
....

4 egg whites

1 cup plus 2 tablespoons superfine sugar
us 1 cup) caster sugar

1 teaspoon vinegar

1 cup quark

1 cup heavy cream

For the Florentine

6 tablespoons sugar

⅔ cup chopped hazelnuts

¾ cup sliced almonds

For the carmelized pineapple

½ cup sugar

1 cup water

1 small, ripe pineapple, peeled, cored &
thinly sliced into rings

In this sumptuous dessert, crushed caramelized nuts are folded into a quark and whipped cream mixture which is used to fill meringue shells. The pavlovas are then decorated with candied pineapple rings. The recipe looks quite complicated, but all the separate components can be prepared well in advance and then put together shortly before serving.

The pavlovas can be prepared a day in advance. Preheat the oven to 225°F. Whisk the egg whites until they form stiff peaks and then gradually whisk in two-thirds of the superfine sugar and the vinegar. Fold in the rest of the superfine sugar. Take 6 metal rings, each 3 inches in diameter, place them on a baking sheet, and fill with the meringue (alternatively, pipe it into disks on parchment paper). Carefully remove the disks. Bake the meringues for 1–1½ hours, until crisp on the outside. Let cool in the turned-off oven.

For the Florentine, put the sugar in a heavy-based pan and melt over a medium heat, then raise the heat and cook until the sugar syrup is a deep golden brown. Stir in the nuts with a wooden spoon. Pour the mixture onto a lightly oiled baking sheet, spreading it evenly, and let cool until hard. Place the nut caramel in a small plastic bag and crush to large crumbs with the end of a rolling pin – or use a food processor.

For the caramelized pineapple, bring the sugar and water to a boil. Add the pineapple rings, reduce the heat, and cook gently for about 30–45 minutes, until the pineapple becomes translucent. Let cool in the syrup.

Whisk the quark and cream together until thick, then fold in the crushed Florentine, reserving about 2 tablespoons to decorate the pavlovas.

To serve, turn the meringues over and carefully scoop out the center from the base of each one, leaving a thin shell. Fill them with the quark cream and turn right-side up again. Place on individual serving plates and decorate with the slices of pineapple. Drizzle the pineapple syrup over and sprinkle with the reserved Florentine.

Chocolate Mascarpone Brûlée

SERVES 4

2 cups mascarpone cheese
1 cup granulated sugar
6 egg yolks
2 ounces bittersweet chocolate
Confectioners' sugar, for dusting

This looks like a classic crème brûlée, *but when you shatter the crisp caramel topping a thin layer of dark chocolate is revealed underneath. You could put a handful of raspberries at the bottom of each dish for another unexpected treat.*

Preheat the oven to 275°F. Lightly whisk together the cheese, two-thirds of the granulated sugar, and all the egg yolks and then strain through a sieve. Pour the mixture into 4 ramekins and place them on a wad of newspaper in a roasting pan (the paper prevents the mixture at the bottom of the dishes getting too hot). Pour boiling water into the roasting pan to come halfway up the sides of each dish and bake for 30–35 minutes, or until the custards are just firm to the touch. Remove from the oven, take the dishes out of the roasting pan and let cool, then chill thoroughly.

Melt the chocolate and spread it evenly over each mascarpone custard. Return them to the refrigerator to chill for 15 minutes so the chocolate sets hard, then sprinkle the remaining granulated sugar over the top. Place under the broiler, close to the heat source, until the sugar is golden and bubbling, then let cool. Dust the edges with a little confectioners' sugar before serving.

P.G.TIPS

A very effective method is to use a small domestic blowtorch to glaze the *brûlées* instead of putting them under the broiler.

Poached Figs Stuffed with Sainte-Maure Cheese in Merlot Wine Syrup

16 ripe but firm figs
4 ounces Sainte-Maure goat cheese
¼ cup mascarpone cheese
Grated zest of 1 lemon
2 tablespoons sugar

For the syrup
½ cup sugar
1 bottle of Merlot (or other red wine)
1 cinnamon stick

ALTERNATIVE
CHEESES

Any soft goat cheese, such as mild Ribblesdale or Montrachet. The Australian Kervella goat ricotta makes an interesting alternative.

Purple figs are best for this dish. During the summer I like to serve some fresh berries sprinkled around the figs.

For the syrup, put the sugar, wine, and cinnamon in a saucepan that is just large enough to hold the figs in a single layer. Bring slowly to a boil, stirring to dissolve the sugar, and simmer for 4–5 minutes. Add the figs and poach for 4–5 minutes, or until just tender. Remove the figs with a slotted spoon. Boil the syrup until reduced to half its original volume.

Purée 4 of the figs in a blender, adding enough of the reduced poaching syrup to give a saucelike consistency. Strain and chill.

Beat together the Sainte-Maure, mascarpone, lemon zest, and sugar. Slice the tops off the 12 remaining figs, fill with the cheese mixture, and replace the tops. Arrange the figs on 4 serving plates, pour the sauce around, and serve.

Pepper-Caramel Roasted Pears with Labna

SERVES 4

1 cup live strained plain yogurt

½ teaspoon ground cinnamon

⅔ cup packed brown sugar

¾ cup water

1 cinnamon stick, broken into 3 pieces

¼ teaspoon cracked black pepper (see Tip on page 146)

4 ripe but firm Bartlett pears

4 tablespoons unsalted butter

⅓ cup Poire Williams or brandy

ALTERNATIVE
CHEESES

A blue cheese or ricotta also goes well with the pears.

The caramel offsets the sharpness of the yogurt cheese, resulting in a simple dessert with complex flavors. This is really quite a straightforward recipe, but you need to start preparations 3–4 days in advance, in order to drain the yogurt for the labna.

Mix the thick yogurt with the ground cinnamon and then drain it in cheesecloth for 3–4 days, as described in the recipe for Labna on page 185.

Preheat the oven to 350°F. Put the sugar in a heavy-based saucepan and leave over a low heat until melted. Raise the heat until it has caramelized lightly, then carefully pour in the water (the syrup may splutter). Add the cinnamon stick and cracked black pepper. Boil for 10–12 minutes to form a light syrup.

Peel the pears carefully so as to keep their shape, then cut them in half, leaving the stems intact. Remove the cores.

Heat the butter in a large, shallow casserole or an ovenproof frying pan, add the pear halves, flat-side down, and cook until lightly colored. Pour over the Poire William's or brandy, turn the pears over, then pour the syrup over. Transfer to the oven and bake for 40 minutes, basting the pears with the syrup once or twice to form a light glaze. Remove from the oven and let cool to room temperature. To serve, top each pear half with a scoop of the labna.

Quark, Prune & White Chocolate Tart

SERVES 4–6

½ quantity of sweet pastry (see page 21)

4 ounces white chocolate

2 gelatin leaves

¼ cup dry white wine

Juice & grated zest of 1 orange

4 egg yolks

2 tablespoons sugar

½ heaped cup quark

⅔ cup heavy cream, semi-whipped

10 prunes, soaked overnight in
¼ cup Armagnac or brandy

ALTERNATIVE

CHEESE

Any curd cheese

Try to get really good prunes for this, preferably French Agen prunes or the large, moist Californian prunes. I like to serve the tart with a fresh orange sauce, such as the one with My Favorite Pick-Me-Up on page 152.

Preheat the oven to 375°F. Roll out the pastry and use to line an 8-inch tart pan. Line with parchment paper, fill with ceramic baking beans and bake for 8–10 minutes. Remove the paper and beans, and bake for a further 5 minutes. Take out of the oven and let cool.

Melt the white chocolate in a small bowl set over a pan of hot water. Brush the bottom of the cooled pastry shell with about two-thirds of the melted chocolate and set aside.

Cover the gelatin leaves with a little water and let soak for 5 minutes. Bring the wine, orange juice, and zest to a boil in a pan. Whisk together the egg yolks and sugar in a bowl for 2–3 minutes, until creamy. Gradually pour the wine and orange mixture onto the yolks, whisking all the time. Cool slightly, then add the soaked and drained gelatin leaves and stir until completely melted. Fold in the remaining melted chocolate.

When the mixture is almost cold and just beginning to set, gently but thoroughly fold in the quark and the semi-whipped cream. Arrange the prunes in the pastry case, then pour in the filling. Chill for at least 2 hours for it to set.

P.G.TIPS
Don't serve the tart too cold, as this impairs the flavor. Remove it from the refrigerator and bring it to room temperature about 15 minutes before serving.

Dried Fruit & Mascarpone Fool with Saffron & Ginger Syrup

SERVES 6-8

1 pound dried apricots

2½ cups water

1 cup mixed dried fruit,
such as apricots, prunes & figs, cut into
large pieces

½ cup sugar

Juice & grated zest of 1 lemon

6 tablespoons apricot brandy (or orange
liqueur such as Cointreau or Grand
Marnier)

1¼ cups heavy cream

½ cup mascarpone cheese

Sprigs of fresh mint, to decorate
(optional)

For the saffron & ginger syrup

2 tablespoons syrup from a jar of candied
stem ginger

Juice & grated zest of 1 orange

1 cup water

A large pinch of saffron strands

I devised this recipe for the Christmas edition of the BBC Vegetarian Good Food *magazine, when looking for an alternative to the traditional Christmas plum pudding.*

Put the dried apricots in a saucepan, pour the water over, and let soak overnight. Bring all the ingredients for the saffron and ginger syrup to a boil, pour it over the mixed dried fruit, and let that soak overnight too.

The next day, bring the dried apricots to a boil, then reduce the heat and simmer for 20–25 minutes until soft, adding a little more water if necessary. Transfer to a blender and add the sugar, lemon juice and zest, and apricot brandy. Blitz to a smooth purée. Let cool.

Whip the cream until it is just beginning to thicken. Beat the mascarpone just to soften it and then fold it gently into the cream. Fold two-thirds of the apricot purée into this mixture. Pour the fool into tall glasses to half-fill them. Put a spoonful of the remaining apricot purée on top and then add more fool, until the mixture is ¾ inch below the rim of the glasses. Chill for 4 hours.

To serve, top up the glasses with the mixed dried fruit in syrup and decorate with the mint sprigs, if using.

Wild Loganberry & Roasted Hazelnut Cheesecake

2 eggs, separated

½ cup sugar

8 ounces wild loganberries (about 1½ cups), plus a few extra to decorate

2 gelatin leaves

1½ cups full-fat cream cheese

⅔ cup heavy cream, semi-whipped

For the base

1 packed cup graham-cracker crumbs

2 tablespoons raw brown or light brown sugar

3 tablespons chopped roasted hazelnuts (see Tip on page 73)

4 tablespoons unsalted butter, melted

For the sauce

8 ounces wild loganberries (about 1½ cups)

Juice of 1 lemon, or to taste

Sugar, to taste

No book on cheese cookery would be complete without a recipe for cheesecake. I prefer the uncooked variety, so here is one of my favorites that I make at home, using autumn produce. If you can't get wild loganberries, try blackberries, blueberries, or raspberries, or a mixture.

For the base, put the graham-cracker crumbs in a bowl and stir in the brown sugar, chopped hazelnuts, and melted butter. The mixture should be sticky but not wet. Press it firmly over the bottom of an 8-inch springform cake pan.

Put the egg yolks and sugar in a bowl set over a pan of simmering water, making sure the water is not touching the base of the bowl. Whisk with a portable electric mixer until the mixture is thick and creamy in color; the beaters should leave a trail on the surface when lifted. Remove the bowl from the pan of water and let cool, whisking occasionally.

Purée the loganberries in a blender and then push through a fine sieve. Put the gelatin in a pan with 3 tablespoons water and leave for 5 minutes, then place over a very low heat until melted and clear. Mix the puréed loganberries with the egg yolk mixture, then stir in the melted gelatin. Add the cream cheese and mix in thoroughly. Whisk the egg whites until stiff and fold them in. Finally, fold in the whipped cream. Pour the mixture into the cake pan and smooth the top with a metal spatula. Chill for at least 2 hours, until set.

Meanwhile, make the sauce. Put the loganberries in a blender with the lemon juice and a little sugar and blitz until smooth. Pass through a fine sieve and add a little more lemon juice or sugar to taste, if necessary. Serve the cheesecake with the sauce, decorated with a few extra loganberries, if desired.

Caramelized Pastry Wafers with Blackberry Crémet

SERVES 4

1 cup cream cheese or fromage blanc

1 cup heavy cream or crème fraîche, semi-whipped

2 egg whites

2 tablespoons granulated sugar

4 ounces puff pastry

¾ cup confectioners' sugar

For the blackberry purée

8 ounces fresh blackberries (about 1½ cups)

½ cup sugar

A little lemon juice

Here, the famous crémet d'Anjou *mixture of cream and soft cheese is blended with a tart blackberry purée and used as a filling between caramelized pastry wafers. It is quite some combination.*

Put the cream cheese or fromage blanc in a bowl and beat until smooth, then fold in the whipped cream or crème fraîche. Whisk the egg whites until they form stiff peaks. Fold in the sugar and then fold the egg whites into the cream cheese mixture. Set aside.

Put half of the blackberries in a blender, add the sugar, and blitz to a purée. Transfer to a bowl and balance the sweetness with a squeeze of lemon juice. Add half the purée to the cheese mixture and gently fold it through to give a marbled effect. Cover and refrigerate for about 12 hours, preferably overnight.

Preheat the oven to 425°F. For the pastry wafers, roll out the puff pastry in a rectangle about 6 by 10 inches and approximately ¹⁄₁₆ inch thick. Dust with a little of the confectioners' sugar, then roll it up very tightly like a jelly roll. Place in a very cold refrigerator or a freezer for a short while to firm up, then with a sharp knife cut the roll into 12 slices about ¼ inch thick. (You won't need all the pastry, but you can freeze the rest for later use.) Liberally dust the slices with the remaining confectioners' sugar and roll them out as thinly as possible into ovals. Place them on a baking sheet and bake for 8–10 minutes, or until golden and caramelized. Remove from the oven and place on a wire rack to cool.

To serve, put a wafer on each of 4 serving plates and cover with some of the marbled cheese mixture. Place another wafer on top, cover with more cheese mixture, then top with a final wafer. Stir the remaining blackberries into the remaining purée and arrange around the wafer stacks.

P.G.TIPS Pipe the cheese mixture over the pastry wafers for a professional finish. These crisp pastry wafers are also good as an accompaniment to ice cream or sorbet. They keep for up to a week in a sealed container in a dry, cool place.

Summer Fruit Gratin with Apricot Stilton Sauce

SERVES 4

8 ounces fresh blackberries
(about 1½ cups)

¼ cup sugar, or to taste

1 pounc mixed fresh summer berries,
such as strawberries, blackberries,
raspberries, red currants (about 3 cups)

For the sauce

⅓ cup heavy cream

¾ cup grated white apricot Stilton cheese

2 egg yolks

¼ cup sugar

Kirsch, to taste

ALTERNATIVE CHEESES

Any cream cheese could be substituted
for the Stilton

I love the refreshing taste of these summer berries, offset with a sweet cheese sauce. Other fruit such as apricots or peaches can be used, or even poached pears during the colder months. Why not try serving the apricot Stilton sauce as a fondue for dipping fruits? In this case, a little apricot brandy could be added instead of kirsch.

Place the blackberries in a blender with the sugar and blitz to a purée. Strain the purée through a fine sieve to remove the seeds. Taste and add more sugar, if desired.

For the sauce, bring the cream to a boil in a pan, then remove from the heat and stir in the cheese. Let cool. Put the egg yolks and sugar in a bowl set over a pan of simmering water, making sure the water does not touch the base of the bowl. Whisk until the mixture becomes pale and thick and doubles in volume. Remove the bowl from the heat and continue to whisk until the mixture is cold. Fold in the cheese and cream mixture and then add kirsch to taste.

Toss the mixed berries with the blackberry purée and pile them up in the center of 4 heatproof serving plates. Carefully pour the cheese sauce around the fruit and put the plates under the broiler to glaze the cheese sauce until light golden in color. Serve immediately.

Lemon Blini with Ricotta & Raspberries

SERVES 4

1½ tablespoons granulated sugar

Finely grated zest of 1 lemon

¾ cup self-rising flour

½ teaspoon baking powder

2 teaspoons melted butter

⅔ cup milk

2 eggs, separated

A pinch each of salt & sugar

1 tablespoon olive oil

¼ cup ricotta cheese, drained

8 ounces fresh raspberries (about 2 cups)

Confectioners' sugar, for dusting

Sprigs of fresh mint, to decorate
(optional)

For the sauce

8 ounces fresh raspberries (about 2 cups)

Juice of ½ lemon, or to taste

¾ cup confectioners' sugar, or to taste

ALTERNATIVE

CHEESE

Quark

A simple, light, lemon-scented pancake topped with ricotta and fresh raspberries and served with raspberry sauce. I like it for dessert with a scoop of vanilla ice cream, but it also makes an excellent brunch dish. For a winter version you could fill the blini with poached pears instead of raspberries. To make chocolate blini, replace 2 tablespoons of the flour with unsweetened cocoa powder.

For the blini, mix together the sugar and lemon zest to extract the lemon's natural oils. Sift the flour and baking powder into a bowl and stir in the sugar mixture. In a separate bowl, whisk together the melted butter, milk, and egg yolks, then combine with the flour to make a batter. Whisk the egg whites with a pinch of salt and sugar until they form stiff peaks, then fold them into the batter. Let stand for 5–10 minutes.

Meanwhile, make the sauce. Purée the raspberries in a blender, then press them through a fine sieve. Stir in the lemon juice and confectioners' sugar, adjusting the quantities to taste if necessary.

To cook the blini, heat the olive oil in a heavy-based frying pan over a gentle heat (or individual blini pans if you happen to have them). Then drop in 2 tablespoons of batter for each pancake so that they are about 4 inches in diameter. Cook for about 2 minutes, until bubbles start to appear on the surface, then flip them over and cook the other side. Keep them warm while you cook the remaining blini—you need 8 in all.

Carefully spread the ricotta over 4 of the blini, then cover with the raspberries. Top with the other 4 blini and put on serving plates. Dust with confectioners' sugar, pour the raspberry sauce around, and serve, decorated with sprigs of mint, if desired.

P.G. TIPS

I've found that boxed pancake and waffle mixes make a good alternative to the flour and baking powder, producing soft, light pancakes.

Corsican-Style Goat Cheese & Honey Omelette

SERVES 4

6 eggs, beaten

1 tablespoon chopped fresh mint

⅓ cup granulated sugar

⅔ cup ground almonds

4 tablespoons unsalted butter

3 ounces soft goat cheese, such as Roubiliac, thinly sliced

2 tablespoons honey

Confectioners' sugar, for dusting

Corsican food is typically Mediterranean, but has a few distinctive hallmarks, one of which is the use of Broccio, a sheep's milk cheese. Broccio is popular in savory dishes and desserts such as fritters, custards, and this simple omelet. It's quite hard to obtain elsewhere, so I have substituted goat cheese, which I actually prefer.

Put the eggs in a bowl with the mint, sugar, ground almonds, and 1 tablespoon cold water and beat until light and fluffy. Heat the butter in an 8 inch omelet pan. When it is foaming, pour in the beaten eggs and stir with a fork. When half set, arrange the goat cheese slices over the top. Let soften slightly, then spoon the honey over and fold the omelet—or leave it flat, if you prefer. Dust with confectioners' sugar and serve warm.

Spiced Apple & Wensleydale Pie

SERVES 4

1 pound apples, peeled, cored & chopped (about 4 cups)

A pinch of ground cloves

1 teaspoon ground cinnamon

A pinch of freshly grated nutmeg

⅓ cup raisins

½ cup sugar

½ cup Wensleydale cheese, broken into small chunks

½ quantity of basic pie pastry (see page 21)

1 egg beaten with 1 tablespoon water, to glaze

Wensleydale cheese should be eaten young and fresh, and is delicious with crisp autumn fruits such as apples and pears. This pie is one of my favorite old English desserts, a traditional Yorkshire way of combining apples and cheese. In this recipe the cheese is mixed with the apples for the filling, but often it is included in the pastry instead. Another Yorkshire custom is to serve a good wedge of crumbly Wensleydale with a slice of rich fruit cake or a mincemeat tartlet. They both offset the cheese magnificently.

Preheat the oven to 400°F. Mix together the apples, spices, raisins, sugar ,and cheese and place in an 8-inch deep dish pie pan. Roll out the pastry a little larger than the pie pan. Cut a thin strip from around the edge and press it onto the rim of the pan, then brush with a little of the beaten egg. Cover the pie with the pastry, pressing it onto the rim and trimming the edges. Flute the edges neatly and make a hole in the center.

Roll out the pastry trimmings and cut out leaves or whatever shape you like. Use to decorate the pie. Brush all over with the beaten egg and bake for 15–20 minutes, until the pastry is golden. Reduce the oven temperature to 325°F and bake for a further 25 minutes. Serve hot or warm, with a light custard sauce or thick whipped cream.

Hot Prune Soufflé with Goat Cheese Ice Cream

SERVES 4

½ cup pitted prunes, preferably Agen prunes

3 tablespoons unsalted butter, plus extra for greasing

3½ tablespoons all-purpose plain flour

1 cup milk, boiled & strained

5 eggs, separated

2 tablespoons Armagnac

½ cup superfine sugar, plus extra for dusting

2 tablespoons cornstarch

4 scoops of Goat Cheese Ice Cream (see page 154)

When we were creating recipes for this book, my sous-chefs and I came across many remarkable combinations that pleasantly surprised us. None more so than this recipe pairing prune soufflé with goat cheese ice cream, which has turned out to be one of my favorites. Try it, and I think you'll see why.

Lightly butter 4 soufflé dishes, each 1 cup in capacity, and then dust with a little sugar, shaking out any excess. Preheat the oven to 400°F.

Simmer the prunes in water to cover until soft. Purée them in a blender and set aside. Melt the butter in a saucepan, stir in the flour, and cook for 1–2 minutes. Gradually stir in the milk to form a thick sauce and simmer for 5 minutes. Stir in the prune purée, remove from the heat, and let cool. Beat in the egg yolks and Armagnac.

Whisk the egg whites until they form stiff peaks, then gradually whisk in the sugar. Finally, whisk in the cornstarch. Beat a third of the egg whites into the prune sauce and then gently fold in the rest. Pour the mixture into the soufflé dishes and put them in a roasting pan containing enough water to come two-thirds of the way up the sides of the dishes. Bake for 15–20 minutes, until well risen. Serve immediately, with the ice cream on the side.

P.G.TIPS A nice touch is to break open the soufflés at the table and put a scoop of the goat cheese ice cream in the center of each one. You could also make extra prune purée and drizzle it over the ice cream.

Apple Pecorino Strudel

SERVES 6–8

1 cup fresh white bread crumbs

½ cup ground almonds

½ cup unsalted butter

2 pounds apples, peeled, cored & thinly sliced (about 8 cups)

¼ cup granulated sugar

1 teaspoon ground cinnamon

½ teaspoon apple-pie spice

⅓ cup raisins, soaked in water until plump

¼ cup chopped walnuts or almonds

Grated zest of ½ lemon

5 ounces pecorino Romano cheese, thinly sliced

4 large sheets of phyllo pastry, each about 18 by 12 inches

Confectioners' sugar, for dusting

ALTERNATIVE

CHEESE

Ricotta makes a tasty alternative to the pecorino.

Another variation on the cheese and apple pie theme (see Spiced Apple and Wensleydale Pie on page 172), this time with an Italian flavor. A simple dollop of whipped cream is all you need to accompany it, but if you prefer something a little more elaborate, try a compote of plums or prunes. Strudel pastry can be time-consuming to make, but phyllo is generally accepted as a convenient substitute nowadays.

Preheat the oven to 400°F. Fry the bread crumbs and ground almonds in 4 tablespoons of the butter until lightly golden, then set aside.

Mix together the apples, granulated sugar, cinnamon, apple-pie spice, raisins, nuts, and lemon zest. Carefully fold in the pecorino cheese.

Melt the remaining butter. Lay out 1 sheet of phyllo on a work surface and brush with some of the butter, then top with the remaining sheets of phyllo, brushing with butter between the layers. Brush the final sheet of pastry with more butter and sprinkle the fried bread crumb mixture over the top. Spread the apple mixture over the surface, then roll up the pastry to form a compact roll. Transfer to a greased baking sheet, curving the strudel to fit if necessary, and brush with the remaining melted butter. Bake for 20–25 minutes, until crisp and golden.

Remove from the oven, dust generously with confectioners' sugar, and serve hot.

P.G.TIPS

If your phyllo pastry is smaller than the size given in the recipe, use extra sheets and lay them out on the work surface, overlapping the edges, to form a rectangle about 8 by 12 inches. Cover with a few more sheets to make 4 layers, brushing with melted butter as above.

Cream Cheese Beignets with Walnut Honey

SERVES 4–6

1 pound cream cheese
2 tablespoons granulated sugar
Grated zest of ½ lemon
1 cup all-purpose flour, sifted
2 eggs
Vegetable oil, for deep-frying
⅔ cup honey
¾ cup chopped walnuts
Confectioners sugar, for dusting

These beignets are one of those sticky, Middle Eastern-style desserts with lots of honey and nuts. Rather than the usual heavy pastries, however, they are light and fluffy little fritters.

Put the cheese, granulated sugar, and lemon zest in a bowl and beat together until smooth. Stir in the flour a little at a time, until thoroughly combined. Beat in the eggs one at a time, then let stand for up to 1 hour.

Put vegetable oil in a deep fryer or large saucepan and heat to 375°F. Drop heaped teaspoonfuls of the cheese mixture into the hot oil, a few at a time, and fry for about 2 minutes, until golden and puffed up. Drain on paper towels and keep warm while you cook the rest.

Heat the honey and walnuts in a pan until just warm. Dust the cheese *beignets* with confectioners' sugar and serve with the walnut honey alongside.

Gorgonzola & Pecan Pie

SERVES 4

½ quantity of sweet pastry (see page 21)
Flour, for dusting
5 tablespoons unsalted butter
¾ cup golden syrup or light corn syrup
4 ounces Gorgonzola cheese, cut into small cubes (about 1 cup)
¾ cup packed light brown sugar
3 eggs
2 tablespoons rum
½ teaspoon vanilla extract
A pinch of salt
1 heaped cup pecan halves

ALTERNATIVE
CHEESE

If you prefer a stronger cheese, you could use Roquefort.

Pecan pie is, deservedly, a universal favorite. The addition of blue cheese makes an interesting variation. I like to serve the pie warm with whipped cream.

Preheat the oven to 375°F. Roll out the pastry on a lightly floured surface until it is ⅛ inch thick and use to line a 9-inch tart pan that is 1 inch deep. Prick the bottom with a fork, line with parchment paper, and fill with ceramic baking beans. Bake for 10 minutes, then remove the paper and beans and bake for a further 5 minutes. Remove from the oven and reduce the temperature to 350°F.

Heat the butter and syrup in a pan, add half the cheese, and stir until melted. In a bowl, whisk together the sugar, eggs, rum, vanilla, and salt. Add the pecans and then stir into the syrup and cheese mixture. Add the remaining cheese and pour the mixture into the pastry shell. Bake for about 30 minutes, until just set.

Croque Mademoiselle

SERVES 4

½ cup Neufchâtel cheese

1 tablespoon Grand Marnier

Grated zest of ½ orange

3 tablespoons grnaulated sugar

8 slices of brioche (see page 22), crusts removed

8 ounces raspberries (about 2 cups)

2 eggs, beaten

⅔ cup heavy cream

⅔ cup milk

1 teaspoon ground cinnamon

4 tablespoons unsalted butter

Confectioners' sugar, for dusting

ALTERNATIVE

CHEESES

Amereican neufchâtel, quark, or firm ricotta

Made with Neufchâtel cheese, this delicate, sweet version of croque monsieur is not unlike pain perdu, or French toast. Although it can be served for dessert, it also makes a good brunch dish or summer breakfast. If possible, use the creamy, fresh-tasting French Neufchâtel.

Mix together the Neufchâtel, Grand Marnier, orange zest, and 1 tablespoon of the sugar. Spread this mixture evenly over the slices of brioche. Top 4 slices with the raspberries, packing them tightly into the cheese, then put the remaining slices of brioche on top.

Beat together the eggs, cream, milk, cinnamon, and remaining sugar and pour into a shallow dish. Dip the sandwiches into this mixture on both sides. Heat the butter in a large frying pan and cook the sandwiches for about 2 minutes on each side, until golden. Remove and drain on paper towels, then dust liberally with confectioners' sugar. Serve the *Croques Mademoiselles* immediately, with some lightly whipped cream.

P.G.TIPS You could substitute white bread for the brioche, although the flavor won't be quite as good. Some supermarkets stock light toast breads, which would work better than plain white bread.

Tourte de Poitou

SERVES 6

½ quantity of sweet pastry (see page 21)

Flour, for dusting

6 ounces soft, unsalted goat cheese, such as Sainte-Maure

3 eggs

½ cup sugar

2 tablespoons heavy cream

3 tablespoons minced candied fruit

Grated zest of 1 orange

1 tablespoon pistachio nuts, skinned & chopped (see Tip)

This tart is a specialty of the Poitou region in France, where it is made with goat cheese, as below. You could substitute cream cheese, if you prefer.

Preheat the oven to 375°F. Roll out the pastry on a lightly floured surface until it is ⅛ inch thick and use to line an 8-inch tart pan. Prick the bottom with a fork, line with parchment paper, and fill with ceramic baking beans. Bake for 10 minutes, then remove the paper and beans and return to the oven to bake for 5 minutes longer.

Meanwhile, beat together all the remaining ingredients in a bowl until thoroughly combined. Pour into the pastry shell and return to the oven to bake for 45 minutes, until the top is a deep golden brown. Serve warm or, if you prefer, cold.

P.G.TIPS To skin pistachio nuts, put them on a baking sheet in a fairly hot oven for 1–2 minutes, then place them in a clean dish towel and rub gently to loosen the skins. Let cool, then peel off the skins.

Baked Amaretti Peaches with Ricotta & Bitter Chocolate

SERVES 4

1¼ cups dry white wine

¼ cup Amaretto liqueur (optional)

½ cup sugar

½ teaspoon vanilla extract or
1 vanilla bean, split open

4 large, ripe peaches

¼ cup firm ricotta cheese

1 cup amaretti cookies, crushed into
small pieces

2 tablespoons grated bittersweet chocolate

2 tablespoons semi-whipped
heavy cream

Fillings for baked peaches are legion, but this combination of soft, fresh cheese, bitter chocolate, and almond cookies is especially good. Apricots can be prepared in the same way.

Preheat the oven to 425°F. Bring the wine, Amaretto liqueur, if using, sugar, and vanilla to a boil in a pan. Boil for 5 minutes to form a light syrup. Add the peaches and poach for 1 minute. Remove the peaches with a slotted spoon and drain well, then slip off their skins. Cut the peaches in half, following the indentation that runs around their circumference. Twist each peach to loosen both halves and then remove the pit. Using a teaspoon, carefully scoop out a little of the flesh to enlarge the cavity.

In a bowl, mix together the ricotta, crushed amaretti, and chocolate, then fold in the cream. Fill the peach halves with this mixture and place them in a baking dish that is just large enough to hold them in a single layer. Pour a little of the poaching syrup into the dish around the peaches and bake for 5–8 minutes, until golden. Serve immediately, with a good vanilla ice cream.

P.G.TIPS
Freeze any leftover poaching syrup to make a delicately flavored peach sorbet. An ideal way to enjoy this dessert all year round is to buy your peaches in the summer and bottle them in syrup for storing. They are also delicious served in their syrup with vanilla ice cream.

Cretan Sheep's Milk Turnovers with Melted Honey

SERVES 4

1 cup crumbled Greek feta cheese

¼ cup cream cheese

1 egg, beaten

4 tablespoons unsalted butter, softened

¼ teaspoon ground cinnamon

Juice of ¼ lemon

2 tablespoons chopped fresh mint

Vegetable oil, for deep-frying

Confectioners' sugar, for dusting

⅔ cup honey, warmed

⅔ cup crème fraîche (optional)

For the pastry

1⅔ cups all-purpose flour, plus extra for dusting

2 tablespoons sugar

2 tablespoons unsalted butter at room temperature, diced

About ⅔ cup water

This marriage of sweet and salty flavors is common in Mediterranean countries. I like to serve some crème fraîche with the turnovers, which makes for a nice contrast of temperatures.

To make the pastry, sift the flour into a bowl and stir in the sugar, then rub in the butter pieces with your fingertips to give a coarse, sandy texture. Stir in enough water to make a soft, pliable dough. Turn out onto a lightly floured work surface and knead for 4–5 minutes, until smooth and elastic.

Place the feta in a bowl and crush it to a coarse pulp with a fork. Add the cream cheese and egg and beat together until smooth. Next, beat in the butter and cinnamon, then the lemon juice and chopped mint. Set aside in the refrigerator until required.

Roll out the pastry as thinly as possible on a lightly floured surface. Cut out 16–20 rounds with a 3-inch pastry cutter. Put about 1 tablespoon of the feta filling on one half of each pastry round. Brush the edges with water, then fold over and seal well to make turnovers. Place them in the refrigerator for 30 minutes to firm up.

Meanwhile, pour vegetable oil into a deep-fryer or a deep saucepan and heat to 350–375°F. Carefully slip the turnovers into the hot oil, a few at a time, and fry for about 2 minutes or until golden, turning them occasionally. Take out and drain on paper towels to remove excess oil. Keep warm while you fry the remaining turnovers.

Place the turnovers on a serving dish, sift a little confectioner's sugar over and drizzle with warm melted honey. Serve immediately, with crème fraîche, if desired.

P.G.TIPS

Try to find a good Greek honey to use in this recipe. If time is of the essence, you could try using phyllo pastry instead. The result will be almost as good, although the turnovers will be a little crispy.

Chapter Eight

Pressed Cheese with Dried Fruits

SERVES 4

4 crottin de Chavignol or aged Chabis goat cheeses, cut horizontally in half

⅓ cup dried figs cut into quarters

¼ cup prunes cut in half

3 sprigs of fresh thyme

3 bay leaves

6 black peppercorns

6 tablespoons prune eau-de-vie or cognac

Olive oil

Serve this delicious cheese preserve with a good walnut bread.

Place 2 of the cheese halves in a sterilized 500-ml (2-cup) preserving jar and scatter a third each of the figs and prunes over, plus a sprig of thyme, a bay leaf, and 2 peppercorns. Sprinkle with 1½ tablespoons of the eau-de-vie or cognac. Put 2 more cheese halves on top, and repeat these layers until all the ingredients are used up, ending with a layer of cheese and pressing it down well. The cheese should be tightly packed. Sprinkle with the remaining eau-de-vie or cognac. Pour in enough olive oil to cover the cheese and then leave in a cool place, but not the refrigerator, for at least a week. Store in the refrigerator once opened.

Simple Marinated Chèvre in Basil Oil

SERVES 4

4 crottin de Chavignol or aged Chabis
goat cheeses, cut horizontally in half

1 bay leaf

6 black peppercorns, lightly crushed

2 garlic cloves, minced

1 handful of fresh basil leaves

½ cup extra-virgin olive oil, warmed

Salt

ALTERNATIVE

CHEESES

A creamy Camembert or Brie,
cut into slices ½ inch thick,
or Roubiliac goat cheese balls

A quick and simple method of marinating cheese, with basil, olive oil, and garlic. I like to serve it as part of a cheeseboard, although it also makes a good light first course accompanied by a small crisp salad and some bread.

Place the cheese halves in a dish just large enough to hold them in one layer and put the bay leaf and peppercorns on top. Blitz the garlic, basil, and olive oil together in a blender to form a fairly liquid sauce and then season with salt. Pour the basil oil over the cheese, cover, and leave in a cool place for about 6 hours. It will keep for about a week in the refrigerator, but bring to room temperature before serving.

Stuffed Bonchester with Walnuts

SERVES 4

1 Bonchester cheese, not too ripe

2½ ounces fresh goat cheese, such as
Sainte-Maure (about ⅓ cup)

2 tablespoons unsalted butter, softened

⅓ cup chopped walnuts

3 tablespoons heavy cream

Salt & freshly ground black pepper

ALTERNATIVE

CHEESES

Brie or Coulommiers (you will need to
double the filling ingredients if you use
these) or Camembert

This was a popular idea in France when nouvelle cuisine was in vogue. Some Michelin-starred restaurants would serve a Brie that had been stuffed with a mixture of soft cheese and fresh truffles. This cheaper variation uses walnuts, although you could, of course, replace them with truffles.

Slice the Bonchester in half horizontally. Beat together the goat cheese, butter, walnuts, and cream and season with salt and pepper. Spread this mixture over the cut sides of the cheese and then put them back together. Chill in the refrigerator for 2 hours to firm up the filling and then cut into small wedges to serve.

P.G.TIPS Using a hot carving knife to slice the Bonchester will make the job easier. The stuffed Bonchester is particularly delicious served with ripe, fresh figs.

Liptauer

SERVES 4

8 ounces (1 cup) cream cheese, such as
Philadelphia or fresh Explorateur

¼ cup sour cream

4 tablespoons) unsalted butter, softened

2 teaspoons capers, drained

2 canned anchovy fillets, minced

1 tablespoon chopped fresh chives

1 tablespoon mild paprika, plus extra for
dusting

1 teaspoon caraway seeds

½ teaspoon mild mustard

Salt

This cheese dip from Hungary is usually made from a soft sheep's milk cheese, which is not always easy to obtain, so I have substituted cream cheese. Crisp crackers are great with this, although a selection of vegetable crudités is also very good. Liptauer keeps for about a week in the refrigerator.

Blend all the ingredients together briefly in a food processor or beat them together in a bowl. Cover and leave overnight in the refrigerator to let the flavors infuse. To serve, adjust the seasoning if necessary, transfer to a serving dish, and dust the top with a little paprika.

Labna with Oregano & Paprika Oil

SERVES 4

2¼ cups live strained plain yogurt

6 large sprigs of fresh oregano

About 2½ cups olive oil

1 tablespoon paprika

Labna, also known as dry yogurt cheese, is popular throughout the Middle East and can be prepared very simply at home by draining yogurt in a cheesecloth bag. It makes a useful base for savory or sweet dishes (see the recipe for Pepper-Caramel-Roasted Pears on page 162) or can be rolled into balls and preserved in oil, as here. If the labna is too acidic for your taste, try stirring in a tablespoon of lightly whipped cream.

Line a colander with 4 layers of dampened cheesecloth. Pour in the thick yohurt, then tie together the ends of the cheesecloth and hang it up over a bowl. Let drain in a cool place such as an unheated room for 3–4 days. On hot days, you may need to drain it in the refrigerator.

Unwrap the yogurt cheese and roll it into small balls, about 1 inch in diameter. Place them in a sterilized preserving jar, tucking in the sprigs of oregano. Mix the oil with the paprika and pour it over the cheese; make sure it is completely covered. Close the preserving jar and leave in a cool place for at least a week before using. Serve with crusty bread.

Gooseberry & Green Peppercorn Chutney

MAKES about 2 pounds

1½ pounds fresh green or red
gooseberries

2 onions, chopped

1 garlic clove, minced

½ teaspoon mustard powder

1 teaspoon lemon juice

1¼ cups cider vinegar
or white wine vinegar

1 heaped cup raisins

A large pinch of salt

½ to 1½ cups packed light brown sugar

2 tablespoons green peppercorns

Serve this chutney with a selection of cheeses and some crusty bread. If you are using the sweeter red gooseberries, you will need the smaller amount of sugar listed in the ingredients. Although you can store it in preserving jars for months, a good chutney will also keep for one month unsealed in the refrigerator and will, in fact, improve in flavor.

Put the gooseberries, onions, garlic, mustard, and lemon juice in a preserving kettle and pour two-thirds of the vinegar over. Bring to a boil, then reduce the heat and simmer for about 45 minutes, stirring occasionally, until thick. Add the raisins, salt, sugar, and the rest of the vinegar. Stir over a low heat until the sugar has dissolved, then simmer for up to 1 hour, stirring frequently, until thick and syrupy. Stir in the peppercorns, then remove from the heat. Either let cool and then store in the refrigerator for up to a month, or pour immediately into hot sterilized jars, seal, process in boiling-water bath for 10 minutes, and store in a cool, dark place.

Saffron Pear Chutney

MAKES about 2 pounds

2 apples, peeled & grated

½ cup minced onion

1 cup golden raisins

Juice & grated zest of 4 oranges

1½ cups sugar

1 teaspoon ground cinnamon

1 teaspoon freshly grated nutmeg

1 teaspoon cayenne pepper

2 pinches of saffron strands

1½ teaspoons salt

¼ cup grated fresh ginger root

1¼ cups white wine vinegar

1¾ pounds pears, peeled, cored & roughly
chopped (about 6 cups)

12 ounces tomatoes, skinned, seeded
& diced (about 2 cups)

The pears are cooked quite briefly so that they keep their shape, resulting in a nice chunky chutney. This chutney is very good served with a mature farmhouse Cheddar such as Montgomery's or Keen's.

Put all the ingredients except the pears and tomatoes in a preserving kettle and simmer for about 30 minutes, stirring from time to time, until the mixture is reduced to a syrup. It should be thick enough to coat the back of a spoon. Add the pears and tomatoes and cook for a further 10–15 minutes, until the pears are just soft. Pour into hot sterilized jars, seal, and process in a boiling-water bath for 10 minutes, then store in a cool, dark place.

CHEESEBOARD (clockwise from top): CAPRICORN, SAINTE-MAURE, KEEN'S CHEDDAR, GOLDEN CROSS, BOULETTES D'AVESNES, ROQUEFORT SOCIÉTÉ, REBLOCHON

Sweet & Sour Grape Pickle

MAKES about 1 quart

1¾ pounds seedless white or green grapes

10 sprigs of fresh tarragon

2¼ cups champagne vinegar or white wine vinegar

¾ cup honey

1 teaspoon salt

A delicately flavored pickle that makes an interesting accompaniment to cheese. Although this recipe uses white grapes, you could substitute red ones. Remember that good-quality vinegar is essential for making a good pickle.

Wash the grapes well and then dry them. Put them in a large sterilized preserving jar with the sprigs of tarragon. Boil the vinegar and honey together for 2 minutes, then add the salt and pour the mixture over the grapes. Seal the jar immediately. For best results, store in a cool dark place for up to 1 month before opening.

Lanesborough Dried Fig & Fennel Seed Bread

MAKES 1 LOAF

1 cake (0.6 ounce) compressed fresh yeast or 1 package rapid-rise dry yeast

½ cup water

2 cups whole-wheat flour

½ teaspoon salt

1 tablespoon unsalted butter

1 cup dried figs cut into strips about ¼ inch wide

1½ teaspoons fennel seeds

This delicately flavored loaf is one of my favorites and a real winner at the Lanesborough, where we serve it as an accompaniment to our cheese selection. I like it slightly warm with my cheese.

If using fresh yeast, put it in a small bowl, pour on the water, and mix until smooth. Put the flour and salt into another bowl and rub in the butter, then make a well in the center and add the yeast and water mixture. Stir in the flour to form a soft dough. If using dry yeast, stir it into the flour after rubbing in the butter and then pour in the water.

Turn the dough out onto a lightly floured surface and knead for 8–10 minutes, until smooth and elastic. Add the dried figs and fennel seeds and knead for 1 minute longer, until incorporated. Do not overknead the dough at this stage or the figs will disintegrate. Let relax for about 5 minutes, then shape into an oval loaf, place on a greased baking sheet, and cover with a clean damp dish towel. Let rise in a warm place for about 50 minutes, until the loaf has doubled in size.

Preheat the oven to 425°F. Bake the loaf for 30 minutes, or until it is golden brown on top and sounds hollow when tapped on the base. Cool on a wire rack.

BREADS (clockwise from top): STILTON BREAD, MOZZARELLA & SUN-DRIED TOMATO BREAD, LANESBOROUGH DRIED FIG & FENNEL SEED BREAD, CHEDDAR & ONION LOAF, CHEDDAR & ONION LOAF, STILTON BREAD (center)

INDEX

ACKNOWLEDGMENTS

Although I am the author of this book, I am only one of a select team of people who
made *A Passion for Cheese* possible. My sincere thanks go to:
- Jane Middleton, for her superb editing of the manuscript: this is our second book
together and I thank her immensely.
- Photographer Gus Filgate, home economists Louise Pickford, and stylist Penny
Markham who, between them creatively enliven these pages.
- Michael Day and Simon Yorke of the Huge Cheese Company for their invaluable
help and for sharing their wealth of knowledge.
- Fiona Lindsay and Linda Shanks, my agents, for their continued backing
- James and Cathy Lane (Gospel Green) and Kevin and Alison Blunt (Golden Cross)
for giving us the use of their farm to photograph, and to Nic Barlow for the wonderful
shots taken there
- My team of chefs here at The Lanesborough, for their help and daily devotion to
good food
- Finally, a big thank you to Kyle Cathie and Candida Hall for their hard work and
enthusiasm for *A Passion for Cheese*, from its initial concept to the finished article.